DANTE'S PARADISO

Illustrated by Sandow Birk
Text adapted by Sandow Birk and Marcus Sanders

Preface by Peter S. Hawkins
Foreword by Mary Campbell
Introduction by Michael F. Meister, FSC, PhD

CHRONICLE BOOKS
SAN FRANCISCO

Library of Congress Cataloging-in-Publication Data available.

ISBN 0-8118-4720-9

Manufactured in China

Design by Alissar Rayes

Distributed in Canada by Raincoast Books
9050 Shaughnessy Street
Vancouver, British Columbia V6P 6E5

10 9 8 7 6 5 4 3 2 1

Chronicle Books LLC
85 Second Street
San Francisco, California 94105

www.chroniclebooks.com

CONTENTS

PREFACE

"MODERNO USO"
By PETER S. HAWKINS, Boston University

What Would Dante Think? This may not be the first question of most people
perusing the new version of the *Commedia* by Sandow Birk and Marcus Sanders;
it was, however, the one that occurred to me, a professional Dantista, when I
stumbled on Birk's *Inferno* installation in the Koplin Del Rio gallery in Los Angeles.
Dominating the show was the brilliantly colorful painting that now forms the cover
of the large-format paperback—an "adaptation" of a spectacular nineteenth-century
luminist canvas by Frederic Church that affords a vision of Hell as if it were
California on a very bad day. (Mt. Rushmore and what look like the remains of
the World Trade Center are thrown in for good measure.) Two-way, multilane
traffic right out of a Piranesi nightmare snakes along a ruined freeway. Fast-food
signs are jumbled together with junked cars; there are oil-rig dinosaurs and telephone
wires heavy with crows; and, just to one side, a death's head reminds us of what
we already know. The scale is vast, the detailing gemlike, the suffused gold and
orange gorgeous. This may be Hell, but who can turn away? In the left foreground,
two tiny figures perched above the radiant abyss—Virgil and Dante—take it all in.

I then moved from that monumental painting to examine the book-size illustrations
of all thirty-four of *Inferno*'s cantos displayed at eye-level around the gallery. It
required an adjustment to a more intimate scale and to a shift from painterly color
to the engraver's black-and-white; it also invited a conversation with yet another
nineteenth-century artist, Gustave Doré. In each of Birk's pictures I recognized the
high drama of Doré's operatic art: its carefully arranged poses, neoclassical allu-
sions, and shadowy architectural settings. All that swirling Romanticism, however,
had been morphed into the low life of a Los Angeles that was at once banal and
menacing: strip malls, car dealerships, vandalized phone booths, back alleys, and
highway overpasses. This urban wasteland was populated by the contorted gym-
nasts of Doré's *Inferno*, looking less like ravaged sinners than like denizens of a
fitness center gone haywire. It was an extraordinarily layered scene: Dante's damned
souls as Doré imagined them, placed within an antiheroic City of the Angels, and
conjured by a postmodernist with a wicked sense of humor.

In a smaller room adjacent to this display, I found thirty-four cameos, each one
presenting a different canto number, usually in Roman numerals. The identifica-
tion sometimes appeared scrawled as graffiti on storefronts and bathroom walls,

sometimes with the propriety of street signs or advertising logos, sometimes like messages left by someone for nobody in particular. Often you had to hunt down the canto indicators, so much were they part of an urban scene that the eye takes for granted or immediately edits out. The full-page illustrations I had first seen played with the contrast between the serious grandeur of Dante and Doré and the "out there" dimension of Los Angeles: The two-storied inflated Fred Flintstone, flanking a megastore escalator, is Birk's version of the giant (Antaeus) who deposits Virgil and Dante in Hell's lowest circle. The cameos, however, were realistic snapshots, miniature glimpses of city life that did not cry out for attention. Yet, in order to discover the canto's number, you had to take the scene seriously enough to find "CANTO VI" painted on the underside of a skateboard, or "CANTO XX" inscribed on a Super Size fries packet, or an alley door marked "CANTO XIX" that might best be left unopened. It was as if Birk were saying that to locate your whereabouts in Dante's poem, you had to take a long hard look at the metropolitan ephemera all around you. Despite the throwaway character of this world, not everything was, in fact, disposable.

What was it about the show that kept a Dante scholar at it for two hours and provoked me to bother the gallery owner until she gave me the wherewithal to contact the artist? To begin with, the boldness of Sandow Birk's undertaking: At the outset of the new Millennium, here was someone undertaking the challenge of taking on a poem that inspired illustration almost from its appearance in the early fourteenth century. Along with the anonymous illuminators of the Quattrocento manuscripts, and in addition to Doré, these include Sandro Botticelli, William Blake, Salvador Dalí, Leonard Baskin, Barry Moser, Robert Rauschenberg, and Marcel Dzama. What distinguished Sandow Birk from this venerable company was his brash irreverence not so much for the *Inferno* itself but for the sage and serious Dante who had been constructed over the centuries.

And then there was Birk's comprehension that, even though technically a journey through the Catholic afterlife, the *Commedia* is even more an exploration of the here and now. As Erich Auerbach famously recognized, Dante is the poet of the "secular world." The great tradition of Dante illustration has usually taken the poem out of our world and presented it as an alternative universe unto itself. Birk, however, takes his cue from the poet, who constantly made the *Inferno* vivid and relevant to his contemporary readers by referring them to places they knew: this Roman bridge crowded with two-way traffic, that listing Bolognese tower, or the Arsenale in Venice, whose shipyard workers spend the winter months applying hot pitch to make boats seaworthy for spring. Birk's *Inferno* comes to us via the sleazy parts of LA, and presents a vision of a postindustrial America that, like Dante's *Inferno*, is relentlessly urban and in decay. Looking for Hell? It's here and now.

As I worked my way through the exhibit I found myself circling back to Birk's illustration of *Inferno* Canto XXVI. This is the famous canto of Ulysses, in which the honey-tongued spinner of falsehood, reduced to a tongue of fire, draws the pilgrim like a moth to a flame. Dante first sees Ulysses in a crowd of other lights that stretch out below him like fireflies flickering in a summer's meadow. What seems straightforward and benign at first appearance, however, proves to be pure deception: each of the lights conceals a false counselor who once used the gift of language to manipulate and destroy. Birk borrows much of Doré's rendering: the massive rocky ledge where the toga-clad Virgil holds on to Dante, the crevice into which they peer, the shining light that draws the pilgrim into its depth. To this scene Birk, however, brings two new elements. He adds the field of fireflies that Doré ignores, which here becomes the myriad lights of Los Angeles sparkling across the city's basin as seen from above. Then there is the rocky outcrop where Virgil and Dante stand, which turns out to be the steep hillside on which steel girders prop up the nine massive letters of the HOLLYWOOD sign. These LA touches do more than add local color or inspire a laugh of recognition: they suggest (in a humorous rather than a moralistic way) that Hollywood's vast metropolis is all about manipulation of words and images, all about honey-tongued spinners of falsehood.

Less than a year after I saw this March 2003 exhibit there was a copy of the *Inferno* in my hands, an "adaptation" of the poem by Sandow Birk and his colleague Marcus Sanders. Neither of them knows Italian; instead of a fresh translation, therefore, they have taken the work of others and made a prose paraphrase set out on the page like free verse. This format has continued in the *Purgatorio* and *Paradiso* volumes. At times the text reads like a streamlined, poor man's version of translators John Ciardi and Robert Pinsky. Details that appear in these editions as footnotes are now brought succinctly into the poetry, no doubt to make the text less threatening and to afford the convenience of "one stop" reading. Birk and Sanders cut through many a textual thicket, sometimes by ignoring the jungle altogether, sometimes by reducing a complicated description to its plain sense. Lost is the incredible richness of a poem that repays endless rereading; gained is a clear sense of what is going on at any given moment, even in discourse as knotty as Statius on embryology in *Purgatorio* Canto XXVI or Beatrice on moon spots in *Paradiso* Canto II.

In addition to simplifying the text, Birk and Sanders have also conjured a contemporary American, California-inflected youth-speak that has been variously described as "guy inarticulateness," "Valley girl," "laid back," "street slang," and "flat, vernacular, profane, irreverent stoner poetry." Italianists and keepers of the flame are sure to be outraged; on the other hand, young people (along with anyone who prefers the vernacular vulgar) will have a good time—as did a thirtysomething

Italian couple I came upon in a bookstore who, after being force-fed the official Dante in high school, were thrilled to discover Birk and Sanders. "Could it be translated into Italian?" they asked.

The authors speak of their work as an "adaptation"; I think of it as a paraphrase on the order of the 1960s *Cotton Patch* New Testament, which took liberties with another "sacred" text in order to make it accessible to people who would not otherwise pick up the Good Book. There's an "as told to" quality to this venture, or better yet, a sense when reading it that someone has cornered you in a bar or a coffee shop with a tale to tell. This kind of living language can have a very short shelf life, and it may well be that the "whatevers" in this text will go the way of "as *if*" in the 1990s, and therefore appear embarrassingly out of touch to next year's "futura gente." Nonetheless, the effect of their chatty orality is to orient the entire poem in the direction of what critics have called Dante's "addresses" to the reader; that is, to generalize the urgent, immediate sense of those discrete moments in the *Commedia* when Dante speaks directly to the person turning his page in order to counsel, encourage, or chide. Their overall tone is urban "Down Home" or good-natured "No Shit."

What Would Dante Think? The poet produced a treatise, *De vulgari eloquentiae*, in scholarly Latin in order to argue the potential glories of the vernacular; he also famously chose to write his enormous poem not in Latin but in the dialect of Florence—*not* what the learned of the day expected of someone so talented and so ambitious. His frame of reference embraced the depths as well as the heights of human experience, and one can as readily find a fart and an asshole in the *Inferno* as plumb the sublime in the *Paradiso*. Not that the poet's diction is always so easy to place: high up in the celestial spheres, for instance, Dante's great-great-grandfather reassures him that if people don't like his truth-telling, then *"lascia pur grattar dov'è la rogna"* (*Par.* XVII, 129)—let them go scratch where they have the itch. (Oddly, this is an opportunity to register Dante's own pungency that the adaptors miss with their "let those who are/ bothered by it deal with it however they want.")

Twice in the poem Dante uses the phrase "uso moderno" either to indicate the normal manner in which things are done now (*Purg.* XVI, 42), or to refer, in a specifically linguistic context, to the feel of contemporary language (*Purg.* XXVI, 113). This conversational "middle flight" (to invoke the register that Milton said he would *not* employ in his *Paradise Lost*) keeps the narrative rolling along. It can diverge into street talk or into conversational banter; it certainly does not shy away from heavy-going theology or sheer verbal pyrotechnics; but the default diction of the poem is colloquial. This quality of a "modern" living speech is miraculously enhanced by the intricate *terza rima* scheme (aba, bcb) that, rather than imposing a rigid form on the Italian, seems instead to release its energies.

The "middle flight" developed by Birk and Sanders moves back and forth between two registers, as we find at the beginning of *Paradiso* I. The opening lines, an easy paraphrase of the Italian text, are neither more nor less colloquial than the original:

> *The glory of God is everywhere and shines in*
> *all things, flowing through the universe, glowing*
> *stronger in some places and less in others.*

Much changes just a few lines later, however, when Dante addresses Apollo, the classical god of inspiration and companion of the Muses:

> *Apollo, I'm calling on your help to finish off this part.*
> *I'm going to need your inspiration if I'm ever going*
> *to deserve to wear your laurel crown. So far I've*
> *only been asking the Muses up on Mt. Parnassus*
> *to help me write this thing, but I'm gonna need*
> *your help to write about Heaven's arena.*
> *I'll need your music to flow through me like*
> *when Johnny won the golden fiddle in that*
> Devil Went Down to Georgia *country-western song.*

Dante's text, in Allen Mandelbaum's translation, goes like this:

> *O good Apollo, for this final task*
> *make me the vessel of your excellence,*
> *what you, to merit your loved laurel, ask.*
> *Until this point, one of Parnassus' peaks*
> *sufficed for me; but now I face the test,*
> *the agon that is left; I need both crests.*
> *Enter into my breast; within me breathe*
> *the very power you made manifest*
> *when you drew Marsyas out from his limb's sheath.*

Birk and Sanders make these lines conversational, guy to guy. From the get-go, they drop the vocative "O" that signals high rhetoric, and then downshift stylistically: "finish off this part," "to write this thing, I'm gonna need / your help." Whereas Dante let the Muses be inferred from the mention of Mount Parnassus, their home, Birk and Sanders bring them on stage in order to make sure they are in the reader's mind without requiring a footnote's explanation.

What is most noteworthy in these lines is the substitute simile they offer at the end of the passage. Here the classical baggage represented by the ghastly story of

Marsyas—flayed alive by Apollo for having challenged the god to a musical duel—is rejected outright, perhaps because it presents too much backstory and poses too many ambiguities to handle at once. (Why, after all, would a poet ask to be taken out of himself as gruesomely as Marsyas was? Why add the transgressive note at this point in the poem?) Instead of retaining the Ovidian reference—one in a chain of such figures running throughout the *Commedia*—we get a vernacular artist ("Johnny") being filled with a power beyond himself; we are given in the golden fiddle a Country-Western equivalent to the laurel crown; and we are referred to a "native" musical idiom that may well strike a chord with the C&W aficionado (although someone not in the know may be as lost as I was by *Devil Went Down to Georgia* reference).

Irony is the natural element for Birk and Sanders, and therefore they are home free in the *Inferno*, where their exuberant spin on Los Angeles corresponds to Dante's own bittersweet (bordering on savage) relationship to his own basin city, Florence. Hell is meant to be a hall of funhouse mirrors, and nobody (despite the deceptive first take) is supposed to look good for long. *Purgatorio* and *Paradiso*, however, present major problems for the ironist: so much in these canticles asks to be taken straight, to be seen as beautiful and good. To be sure, the city-states of Italy and kingdoms of Europe are still witheringly invoked, warts and all; on the seven terraces of the Mountain we also see how the penitence fits the sin, as when the Proud carry on their backs the stony burden of their egos (depicted by Sandow Birk as men ascending a staircase, doubled over by appliances). Yet Dante's Purgatory is not another exercise in infernal absurdity, but Hell turned inside out and right-side up. In the poet's rendering it is a mountain where pain means gain; it is all outdoors, bathed in sunshine and in the light of stars. Extraordinary natural beauty is matched by the hyperrealistic artwork of God, the "better craftsman" who orchestrates the whole process of transformation through intaglio murals, carved pavements, pageants and processions, and dramas that appear to the mind's eye alone. The hard climb culminates in Eden, a pastoral dream come true, the human "nest" once lost and now regained.

When illustrating the second canticle of the poem, as well as in the paradisiacal third, Birk continues the urban reference of his *Inferno:* his afterlife will always be here and now, in mundane America. Instead of remaining in Los Angeles, however, the city of choice for his Purgatory is San Francisco. This marks a visual upgrade: some use is made of its hilly topography, and there are occasional vistas that open up to the Bay Bridge or the Transamerica Building. But by and large this "second kingdom" is still gritty and urban, kept low to the ground, and alluded to in details that wittily situate us in the Bay Area—we find BART rather than the freeway; there are more Asian take-outs than Latino.

Yet, surprising for a city location that boasts the glorious Golden Gate Park, Birk finds in San Francisco—one of America's most beautiful cities—no analogy to Dante's paradisiacal groves and sparkling waters. Instead, his "Garden of Eden" turns out to be a strip joint in the North Beach neighborhood. Matelda in bikini and heels writhes in a pole dance; the three theological virtues are a trio of hotties named Faith, Hope, and Charity; and the divine Beatrice—Dante's "girl," chubby in a little black dress—walks these mean streets with a don't-mess-with-me attitude. The Dante scholar is puzzled by these choices. Is Eden placed on the wild side of the tracks because the pastoral no longer speaks to us? Does the theological romance that Beatrice represents in the *Commedia* appear too idealized and highfalutin for our "moderno uso"? Are we more likely to entertain the notion of a golden-hearted hooker than imagine a beloved who is at one and the same time herself and Christ? Is our all too solid flesh compelling, reliable, *real*, in ways that the spirit (or whatever) is not? Birk's response to these questions reveals what motivated him to transform Dante's Earthly Paradise into a red-light district: "Beauty and goodness might be found in a strip bar, inspiration in a sunrise; contemplations on the nature of the soul can happen with a homeless person, and the fictional muses of Faith, Hope, and Charity might just as well be represented by the 'hotties' of today as by the 'hotties' of yesterday that we find in Romantic painting."

The third volume of Birk's *Commedia* marks his radical reinvention of Dante's vision. In his *Paradiso* we see most clearly that he is less interested in illustrating Dante than in using him as a starting point for his own vision of the present. Instead of a Beatrice who gets progressively more beautiful as the journey ascends the ladder of being, Dante's "girl" remains the strangely plump figure she was in *Purgatorio*, getting neither younger nor more lovely as she ages: "In any *American* 'Divine Comedy' there have to be fat people." Here beauty lies in the eye of her lover rather than in any beholder of these images. The blessed souls, who are invisible in *Paradiso* because of their effulgence, are rendered by Birk as ordinary folk likely to be found on a New York subway hurtling through Manhattan for destinations in Queens or The Bronx. They are meant to remind us of those who surround us now, ordinary folk without haloes or harps: "the fat, the young, the old, the hip-hop youth and Asian shopkeeper, the garbage truck driver, the businessman." In this paradise the blessed appear as what they were in life, not, as in the original canticle, as invisible creatures of light that the poet-pilgrim encounters, planet by planet, in a succession of luminous configurations: circumscribed circles in the Sun, a cross in Mars, an imperial eagle in Jupiter, a ladder in Saturn, a meadow of flowers in the Heaven of the Fixed Stars. They look like us, no better, no worse.

The irony and wit that characterized Birk's *Inferno* carry on in beatitude, though with less bite. For instance, in the spirit of the HOLLYWOOD sign riding high above Hell's false counselors, Dante's Eagle of Justice in *Paradiso* XVIII–XX becomes a McDonald's "M" hovering over Times Square—*signum imperii* of the United States' global empire—while the six souls who make up its eye are a TV billboard in Tokyo all flashing the image of a "corporate" rock band. As on Earth, so in Heaven.

Doré attempted to capture the ineffable Empyrean through dense swirls of indistinct angels, "ten thousand times ten thousand," revolving around a central luminosity—an empty space, perhaps corresponding to the divine excess that the poet cannot finally articulate. In this image Doré was considerably more successful than elsewhere in his *Paradiso*, whose illustrations have none of the energy and invention of his *Inferno* and largely dissolve into the pious cliché of his times: a plaster-saint Beatrice, a surfeit of diaphanous robes and angel wings. Predictably, Birk will have none of this. His vision of the Cross that Dante glimpses when he ascends to the heaven of Mars (*Paradiso* XIV) is not Doré's crucifix held aloft by a swarm of angels, before which the pilgrim poses reverently on the prie-dieu of a cloud; it is, rather, the sun setting through the crossed supports of the Williamsburg Bridge. Paradise Now, as close as Brooklyn and the Lower East Side.

Most astonishing of all, however, is Birk's rendering of the City of God. For the realm of the imageless ineffable, Dante constructs a metaphoric impossibility that can be "seen" only in motion, in the switching back and forth between antithetical images—an immense white rose and a Coliseum-like amphitheater. In the blurring of quite different worlds of symbolic discourse, the flower of Venus and of Mary, the New Jerusalem and a New Rome "where Christ is a Roman," all come together before fading into the lightning flash that concludes the poem. How to depict this extraordinary synthesis that can last only a moment before language fails, the *Commedia* ends, and the poet finds himself carried into an experience he cannot talk about? Birk's sense of an ending borrows Doré's view of the Empyrean as a swirl of circles around an apparently empty vortex. But in perhaps his most remarkable rethinking of his sources—of Dante's poem as well as of Doré's engravings—the still point of the Empyrean's turning world becomes the Kaaba at the heart of Mecca. We have all seen the photographs: ten thousand times ten thousand of the white-robed devout, who circle the black stone shrine at the center of a plaza, within which lies a sacred black stone said to have been given to Abraham by the archangel Gabriel. This holiest of objects in Islam draws faithful pilgrims from all over the world, many of whom direct their prayers toward it five times a day wherever they may be, and who make Mecca the destination of an obligatory once-in-a-lifetime pilgrimage.

What would Dante think? The poet is notoriously hateful toward Islam, which he saw as an aberration of Christianity that divided the Body of Christ and prevented a unified world empire. Hell's most disgusting punishment is in fact reserved for Mohammed and his son-in-law Ali, who are found in *Inferno* XXVIII among grotesque, Schismatics. They tear into their own bowels and rip open their chests: "See how fucked up I am now?" shouts the Prophet in the Birk-Sanders rendering. Dante's afterlife does not take kindly to other religions! And so the poet consigns the pagan worthies of the ancient pre-Christian world to Limbo, the first circle of Hell, and affirms through the Eagle of Justice that no one ever came to Paradise except by believing in Christ either before or after his Incarnation. Nonetheless, there appear to be loopholes in his well-wrought theological system. Two medieval Muslims take their place in Limbo along with virtuous Greeks and Romans; Cato, a pagan suicide, is guardian of Purgatory; and a Trojan comrade of Aeneas, Ripheus, keeps company with King David in the Heaven of Justice.

Perhaps in giving us his paradisiacal Mecca as the centerpiece of the City of God, Birk is pushing Dante's own envelope, moving him farther along a path he had just begun to blaze in the *Commedia*. There are hints of this earlier on, when the angel who guards the entrance to Purgatory appears against a Hindu temple backdrop or when the cameo art for Canto XXII evokes the religion of the Aztecs. In one sense, of course, the artist is having fun with any form of religious absolutism: "Wouldn't that be a twist if when the Catholics get to heaven, it's a Muslim place?" Birk is also having fun with the Dante who is presumptuous enough to place his "girlfriend" high in the heavenly hierarchy, only a seat or two away from the Virgin Mary! Beatrice's inclusion in *Paradiso* is one of the poet's more unorthodox (not to mention audacious) moments; as such, it may invite the opening of doors that Dante closed tightly or only left ajar. For all the tweaking, Birk's intent is serious: "I would like to imagine a heaven where everyone can go—the Jews, the Muslims, even 'the people from near the Ganges' who have never heard of Jesus."

There is something Dantesque about this taking of liberty with a source. The poet never scrupled to make use of other writers without particular regard for the integrity of their work, just as he invariably rewrote what he read when it suited him. We see this, for instance, almost every time he borrows or even quotes from the *Aeneid*. Again and again we are told that Virgil is Dante's revered mentor in art, that his text is the flame that ignites other poets, that he is a fountain that pours forth like the Muses' springs on Mount Helicon; but this in no way stops the poet from refuting Virgil's essentially tragic vision by writing a Virgilian *Commedia* or from transforming the master's despairing pagan text into a hopeful Christian one. It is not that he misunderstood what Virgil had so beautifully imagined and expressed; it is, rather, that he used an old world to construct something new, something that answered the call of "moderno uso." So too with the efforts of Birk and Sanders: the point should not be to focus on what the adaptation "got wrong" about Dante, but rather to pay attention to what this new world of image and text has to reveal.

FOREWORD

WRATH, ORDER, PARADISE

By MARY CAMPBELL

> *"And you mortals, keep yourselves restrained in*
> *judging; for we, who see God, know not yet all the*
> *elect."*
>
> PARADISO XX, 133–35

During the pre-apocalyptic summer of 1999 I reread Dante's *Commedia* for the first time without notes or commentary at hand. It was an interesting experiment, reading an old, old poem intended to exist outside of its time with neither commentary nor a Dantista's knowledge of Italian micropolitics.

I felt stormy often, as many have before me: for Northrop Frye, the *Inferno* was "the greatest obscenity of the Middle Ages." After the mobility and Eros and orient sapphire of *Purgatorio,* where everyone climbs the same mountain, passing through the same seven territories of reparation at varying speeds, it was raining hard in Heaven when I found again, harder to bear this time, the judgments, placing and fixing human souls in hierarchical order—the first of the blessed Dante meets begins immediately to explain for what fault she has been placed "in the slowest sphere" (*Para.* III, 51).

The ordinal fixation of Dante's spiritual cosmos brings the image of his Paradise into close relation with the oppressive orders of the military, of racial caste (mulatto, quadroon, octoroon), of class. Ordination first, rationalization second. A colleague says to my objections: "But it's still important to keep the *ideal* of justice" and I say, perhaps insanely, No: it is precisely that ideal that wreaks such systemic "miscarriage" of itself in the world, where the ideal cannot be realized and its approximations cannot be just.

The *Commedia* can be read as a transcendental love story, but the texture of the *Paradiso* does not read as though energized by Eros. Dante's writing energy pours into diatribes against various polities and politicians, temporal and spiritual, uttered by those engaged in eyelocks with the very fount of being: Cunizza explains, in the sphere of Venus, that "because her people [Guelfs] are stubborn against duty, Padua at the marsh will stain the waters that bathe Vicenza" (*Para.* IX, 46–48). St. Peter rails, at the brink of the Ninth Heaven, "It was not our purpose that the keys that were committed to me should become the ensign on a banner for warfare against the baptized" (*Para.* XXVII, 49–51), the literal sense an allusion to the papal troop sent against Frederick II in 1229. Into which ring of Hell would I put this compulsive point-counter and grudge-bearer? Into which ring of Hell would he put me?

Is poetry an institution of moral judgment?

Or is judgment just a phase of human consciousness this particular European poem must encompass in its wide Hell-mouth? I am curious—was personal and private judgment once more prevalent, honored, powerful, as an emotion supported by certain high levels of character, than it is now? Or was it just one of the temptations of *auctoritas*? If God was a judge, then so perhaps could Dante be, without shame. But: "judge not, lest ye be judged," saith the Lord. And, "judgment is mine."

The poet's judgments are consequential: consider the effect, on the reputations of his forbears Brunetto Latini and Priscian the Grammarian, of his unsubstantiated accusations of sodomy. Dante should have been singed not on the Cornice of Love but in the Circle of Judges. But there isn't one.

> If [the longitude and latitude of every place] were known, man would be able to know the characteristics of all things in the world and their natures and qualities, which they contract from the force of this location.
> —ROGER BACON, OPUS MAJUS

In the world that preceded print and large personal libraries, the arts of memory helped people manage knowledge by storing it internally on a spatial grid that inevitably saturated its data with hierarchy and allegorical significance. The *Commedia* is what the commemorative spiritual exercises. Ignatius Loyola later called a memory palace, a topographical map of spiritual knowledge like the Tibetan Kalachakra, or the fourteenth-century frescoes of Hell and Heaven in Florence's Santa Maria Novella (where Dante probably attended the studium). The memory palace invites long meditation on the structure and details of its depicted spaces and the beings who occupy them. It is rooted in the notion of the *topos* (Latin *locus*) or "place," as it is known in rhetoric. The architectonics that are the *Commedia*'s grandest effects are then a function of rhetoric, in the service of memory and spiritual experience. They are also, as Roger Bacon tells us, all we need to know to know who and what is in the system of places they construct.

The medieval idea espoused above by Bacon assumes not only a belief in geography as helping to shape individual and ethnic character, but a belief in—or perhaps semiconscious reliance on—judicial astrology, then part of astronomy. Dante's (nondeterminist) belief in the shaping influence of the physical heavens went farther than that of the theologians, despite his deep belief in Free Will. Ideas of geographical and zodiacal influence, understood in Macrobian zone theory to predispose one to certain characteristics or in Foucault's term "resemblances," make easy homologies with an aristocratic society's understanding that estate and social status predetermine, not only one's place *(topos)* at the table, but one's capacities and one's right to power.

This hierarchy of being and power is normatively repudiated by modern liberal democracies, in which individual or national relation to cash flow determines the distribution of rights. It would be easy to indulge in as much "rigid judgment" (*Inf.* XXX, 70) as Dante does in the *Inferno* if the representative personae of the cash nexus were considered for a moment, or their doppelgängers, the politicians they pay for, the shadows of the shadow puppets. The pleasure of imagining shelves of torment for top executives of the World Bank, for Rupert Murdoch, Steve Forbes, or the congressmen who keep Texas oil companies afloat by abolishing social welfare, is palpable. But indulgence of every kind is the name of our weary 2K game. Moralist indulgence is another shadow of the shadow puppetry of wild consumption, wild expansion. A puppetry already begun in the city-states of fourteenth-century Italy. We go to Dante for tact, for order.

Do we like order, then?

Apparently, I do not. This summer Dante reads like a utopianist to me, sinless and omniscient, eager to represent an order that will exclude the messes caused by rebellion, ambition, restlessness, curiosity, desire, even by moral or cultural difference. I cannot bear to be told what is right and wrong in such specific detail, in the zestful context—even in heaven!—of graphically visualized punishments or subordinations.

Why not? In part because I was a "Catholic girl": like Dante, though unwillingly, I still secretly believe the Law is real, the order(s) invoked by its patriarchal operatives and beneficiaries valid, larger than I am, time-honored. I believe, deep down, in the Author, and that he is listening to me read. So it's not enough just to say "how medieval!" and get on with "the poetry."

But order is a difficult theme for diatribe. Start writing about it and it threatens to convert you, by means not only of its heavily armed police but of its religious or supernatural charm, its sentimental charm—its promise to hold you. The famous autistic designer of slaughterhouse equipment, Temple Grandin, intensely empathetic with the cows and pigs she designs her guillotines for, has described the necessity for her of being held, not by a human but in a confining place (a *topos*). She says she understands that cows need and want this too, and in her humanely engineered abattoirs the cows are held tightly and guided individually to their appointed ends.

Dante's immortal and orderly abattoirs are less humane. George Santayana wrote in *Three Philosophical Poems* of the inscription over the gate of Dis: "The damned are damned for the glory of God. This doctrine, I cannot help thinking, is a great disgrace to human nature" (p. 115). Perhaps, but it was no human who inscribed it on that gate. Dante's Paradise represents *God's* fiction, a *didactic* fiction. The souls' inadvertent performance of it is for us—the living, the students; it confirms or enlivens our belief that sin's consequences, life's consequences, are enormous.

The fiction therefore uses, and in so doing might figuratively be said to abuse, the blessed souls who must array themselves in the various *tableaux vivants* of the *Paradiso*'s light show. These formations may not be amenable to the inherently mobile nature of the soul. To explain the pain of purgatorial fire for the immaterial bodies of souls in Purgatory, Thomas Aquinas describes it as a jail: "fire of its nature is able to have an incorporeal spirit united to it as a thing is united to its place . . . as the instrument of Divine justice [the fire] is enabled to detain it enchained."

I do not look forward to participating eternally in a choreographed demonstration, a Busby Berkeley ballet of compelling but tiring force, for the benefit of occasional lost souls. I want joy, huge heaping tons of joy, *compensation*. And I do not want it to be found in some outer ring of the blessed, where I helpfully indicate to tourists that even the Outer Rings are happy: "Our affections, which are kindled solely in the pleasure of the Holy Ghost, rejoice in being conformed to his order" (*Para*. III, 52–54). I want *all happiness*. I did not die under torture or in prison. I have experienced relatively ordinary levels of anguish. And still I want relief, and an apology, although in fact I expect nothing, not even silence.

Dante Alighieri did not live in postmodern America. Perhaps in his particular Italy the rigid placements of social order and a perpetual readiness to judge were to be preferred over an always-threatening level of violent chaos we call an "emergency" when we see it now, in Kosovo or South Central L.A. It is probably better to read his *Inferno* and *Paradiso* as registers of horror at the approaching collapse of empire, papacy and feudalism itself. The concept of order had not yet been corrupted by its associations with Fascism and Apartheid.

At any rate, I am being impossible. Order is a feature of poetry as well as of the cosmos and of the idea of justice. A world-encompassing allegorical poem is necessarily isomorphic with the avatar of world-encompassing order known as Justice,

and if we are enjoying that placing, enclosing, and holding at one level it is diffi-
cult to reject it at the level it mirrors. That's the magic trick of allegory.

No artist can inveigh forever against the "blessed rage for order"—though, *note well*,
it is a *rage*. It is perhaps the meaning of social order as an object of approval or
reverence, and especially the relation of human judgment to order, that have detained
me all this long hot summer. For here are issues of dominance and power and Dante,
whatever his powerlessness in the actual social realm of exile, has all the power in
his poem—including the power of rhetoric to convince, to move, to terrify.

Perhaps in Dante's Heaven and Hell souls go precisely where they want to go, find
their own places. ("What I was living, that am I dead!" yells Capaneus in Hell
[*Inf.* XIV, 51], and Piccarda in "the slowest sphere" of Heaven asserts that "the
power of love quiets our will and makes us wish only for that which we have" [*Para.*
III, 70–72]). It's a wonderful idea; the present Pope has just reaffirmed it. But
though it's declared often, it does not seem to me represented in the *Commedia*,
only declared. Where it is absent, one can easily feel oneself in the presence of a
hanging judge in border country, where "the law's whatever I say it is."

One reads the *Commedia* more literally without commentaries. Whatever else, the
poem is a narrative fiction, narrated by an "I" who is the central character, the
only character with whom a reader can "identify"—in whom we can place our-
selves—as the others disappear continuously. Modern readers can identify with
Virgil for about half of the poem—he is like us in being barred entrance to the
territories of the true aristocrats, the Saved, but he is not "I," the poem rejects
him with no formal leave-taking, and we keep reading.

At any given moment one can (and usually does) "identify" with a soul in torment.
But the only consciousness to whom the whole narrative is as present as it must
be to the reader is that of the "I"—not only a soul developing towards enlighten-
ment, but also the representative of a soul in rage, a soul that defines and creates
the states of torment that are our only alternative to identification with Dante the
revenant narrator. This narrator is an implacable taxonomist, who knows exactly
how much heaven to dole out to whom, who can only imagine the sublime of tran-
scendence as a set of gradations and promotions, of places we will know and keep.

The rage I feel against this narrator, against the idea of order itself, is hard to
control: Justice, says Freud, begins in the nursery, and contemplation of it easily
returns us there. I have been trained to honor Dante as both the most Perfect Poet
of All Time and also the revenant, the man who has seen the country of Death,
and has deserved such a vision. For many Catholics, it is his Afterlife to which we
are all headed. Where we can rest assured we will not have to sit next to a Jew on

the strictly segregated bleachers, and that there will be very few Guelfs, whatever a Guelf is. But we will be held. Held in place, like a cow in an abattoir who never arrives at the blade itself.

I want to protect the dead and the to-be-dead from Dante, because atavistically I feel he has the power to hurt them, and that power must be the power of poetry, since he died banished and poor, in someone else's house. In my miserable millennial nursery I want to rearrange heaven, so everyone will be as close to God as everyone else, and slow learners like Piccarda won't have to stand submissively in the back ("you will see a marvelous correspondence of greater to more, and of smaller to less, in each heaven with respect to its Intelligence," *Para.* XXVIII, 76–78), reading the eyes of God at a third-grade level.

Or better—so that people can take a walk and get away from God, the Great and Powerful. I want to redesign God, so he has some of the enlightened compassion necessary to design a heaven that will in fact, as Robert Thurman says of the Kalachakra, "nurture beings' development" (rather than "fix you," like Eliot's party guest, "sprawling on a pin"). So that he has enough of it to design a hell that will at least not suffer from comparison with Temple Grandin's abattoirs. I want Dante's sister-in-law, Piccarda, abducted from a convent and raped into marriage, to be forgiven for not "escaping" back to the imprisonment that preceded the marriage. I want Dante to spend several lifetimes as a woman, as a Jew, as a Muslim, as a Guelf, as a Black Ghibelline, as a Pope. I want him to burn and weep in the Circle of the Judges.

What an extraordinary matter, that such a poem, such an infinite thing, such a powerful story with so many consequences in the religious imaginations of "those who will call these times ancient," that a poem describing—as no European poem before and perhaps no European poem since has done—Paradise, should be so bitter.

So desperate, so merely personal. What a disappointment, when one had wanted there to be the Poet, the Vision, the Cosmos, the Truth. A home. There's no place, unfortunately, like home. The exile knows that one way, the reader of Dante guesses it another. Home (that "world endlessly bitter" [*Para.* XVII, 112]) is where, if you have to go there, they don't have to take you in after all.

Middle-class modern people tend to respond defensively to the "judgmentalness" of Dante's spiritual world, sensing that Dante would probably at best assign them to the outer suburb of the meaningless, that monotonous crowd doomed to be harried by mosquitos for eternity, rejected even by Satan. Late Capitalist culture has made of us "consumers," an "audience," people who must be attracted, wooed, not threatened and shamed.

People who are used to being as Special as Dante is (central focus of the Eternal World for a whole week!), but who are suspicious of merit, even a sense of their own, lest merit and demerit complicate their/our imagination of "democracy." It is not a heavy task to share the irate Dante's need to place us all on some ratty couch in the leaking Vestibule of Hell's fern bar.

But we are not completely worthless, I think. In a work that promises to introduce us to the "endless variety of goodness," as a friend of mine put it, we are properly disappointed to find instead a hierarchy of goodness, which can only rest justly on the premise of a single conception of goodness, a single axis of achievement. History excuses us from finding submission to the will of God the highest imaginable form of goodness: "God" has too often willed genocide as a response to the disorder of moral difference.

It is not the poet Dante's fault, of course, that those of later days who shared his imperialism, his love of order, his hierarchicalism, his ethical "objectivity," have provided some of history's most appalling monsters. Our world is one in which order has so triumphed that the very *conception* of goodness is in doubt, and many souls of moral dignity have deep ambivalence about the orderly production of beauty as well. After the efficient order of Auschwitz, Adorno feared, any poem—not just a spiritually eugenic poem like the *Commedia*—might be a sin by association with the unspeakable rhymes of the death camps. But Dante's world was closer than ours to being one of sheer, random willfulness. The life of a member of the global village, the global economy, the registry of motor vehicles is a different matter, life now nearly extinguished by an excess of order.

And it is not Dante's fault that I was brought up to feel that order was good, and that art was not order but the subversion of order, and that I too was a misfit in the moral order that constitutes the world's real beauty. Not Dante's fault that so many boys of my generation died or were ruined for the institution of a "new world order," and that they are said to have found restitution now in the beautiful order of Maya Ying Lin's Vietnam Veterans' Memorial in the nation's capital. Not Dante's fault that his *Commedia* was taught in colleges to generation after generation of the powerful, the political class, those for whom that God's-eye view had huge convenience in the necessarily pitiless pursuits of foreign policy, urban redevelopment, criminal justice systems, and the free market. Certainly not Dante's fault that aerial photography, mimicking his visual perspective on the blessed in heaven, has revealed to the twentieth century the astonishing orderly beauty of mass destruction, whether military or industrial.

Dante himself, when not designing God's fiction of Justice for Him, is flinching at it, weeping, trembling, fainting, disappearing in it. He is never angry at it though—it is as if he has left that business to us, whoever he thought we might be. I don't feel guilty toward him for this rage, because his poem has invited it—indeed, invented it. For there is no God, no Afterlife, no three-ring circus of fixed destinies on display. There is only the rhetorician, Dante, and his grand design. A design that includes a suffering subject through whom we can feel the horrors and injustices of Justice, and a thousand objects in whom we can see ourselves—truly dead, like specimens—from the perspective of Justice. Could Dante's *Commedia* be an indictment, not of the human beings Frye commends for having the quiet courage, after this poem, to go on sinning, but of a world in which the greatest imaginable reparation must be this hard to distinguish from the madness of cruelty? Is the *Commedia* a *cri de coeur*, rather than an Encyclopedia of the Cosmos?

Dante slips easily through the Cornice of Wrath, despite the obvious wrath of his composition. In the poetic order of his poem it is necessary for him to be stalled on the Cornice of Lust, where that sin is corrected that impersonates—and underestimates—the fundamental physics of his cosmos. In the fecund disorder of reading it, however, his reader will do his penance for him on the proper cornice. In the awful effectiveness of the poem, this reader's own inadequate idea of "goodness" might even place her in Hell, its fifth, wrathful ring, where Dante should be her company but isn't—because the magic power of Poetry protects him as well as it does the pagan Poets, whose place in Hell is the very Paradise they conceived for their own heroes.

Despite the problems of our resistance, to be in the story ourselves, as I have said before, we must be in it as Dante the protagonist is, because his is the only subjectivity there to inhabit—except for the narrator's, also Dante. Dante trying to find out the particular shape of his own failure to be human, or simply rehearsing the precise shape of his own terror of the world. Or Dante designing an infinite that hurts us, "detains" us, shames us. Narrative entails the danger of knowing through imaginative experience. Dante has made me know, and utter, the utter wrath of the soul who refuses to submit to another.

And in so doing of course I've let the Poet manhandle me, dead though he is, imaginary though he is, enraged though I am at his timidity in suppressing his own subliminal hatred of God. I've let him make me his puppet. He's hurt me, detained me, shamed me. He's brought me inside his imaginary world, though I am real and he no longer is.

The first time I taught the *Commedia*, the sweetest and (I thought) dumbest student in the class said on her course evaluation form that she was grateful to me for having given her back her beautiful religion. I was curious about that for a long time. This summer I am wondering if it wasn't terror that yanked her back into place as a good Catholic girl who could aim without sin for the outer, "slowest" sphere of Blessedness. The terror of someone who had courageously opened herself to Poetry and found it more powerful than Sunday School.

How much does this power have to do with the constantly enacted power of the liturgical word, the *sacramental performatives:* I baptize thee, I renounce thee, Satan, This is my body . . . ? Is the fiercely competitive Dante competing here with his hated popes, and winning? The liturgical is the extreme case of the performative, of language as literally creative, enactive. According to Allen Grossman, the poets are always in competition, not with mere popes but with the gods, those fictioneers whose worlds we are doomed to die in. If the poets win, does that mean they have become as gods?

Premier Dante scholar Charles Singleton's final note to the *Commedia* is touchingly but chillingly atavistic:

> *No poet could have endured a greater tragedy than Dante, had exile and then death at the age of 56 forced him to leave his* Commedia *unfinished—which would have meant that a structure . . . designed to reflect God's work in its completeness and perfection, would have failed in its goal. But at some time before that fatal date of mid-September, 1321, that last verse, speaking of Love to the very end, had been conceived and penned, and that* Comedy *to which Heaven and earth had set hand, and had made its author lean through many years, was done, an "imitation" finished in its perfection.* (2: 609–10)

"That which overcomes you is power against which naught defends itself" (*Para.* XXIII, 35–36). Poetry's power is what Dada and L=A=N=G=U=A=G=E poets have renounced in fierce loathing. Like Procne, they are dicing up the corpse to serve the murderous Father in *contrapasso,* and are silenced and made to sing nonsense syllables. Their resistance is futile, as is that of any resister in Dante's finished, perfected world. They will perhaps go to my heaven, but my heaven is only make-believe. And in it I will be found curled in a sudden arbor, beside a purling stream, my hair lifted by a breeze in which the distant notes of caroling angels drift, reading the *Commedia* and gnashing my teeth.

—This essay first appeared in *The Poets' Dante,* edited by PETER S. HAWKINS and RACHEL JACOFF, published by FARRAR, STRAUS & GIROUX, 2001, and appears here with the publisher's permission.

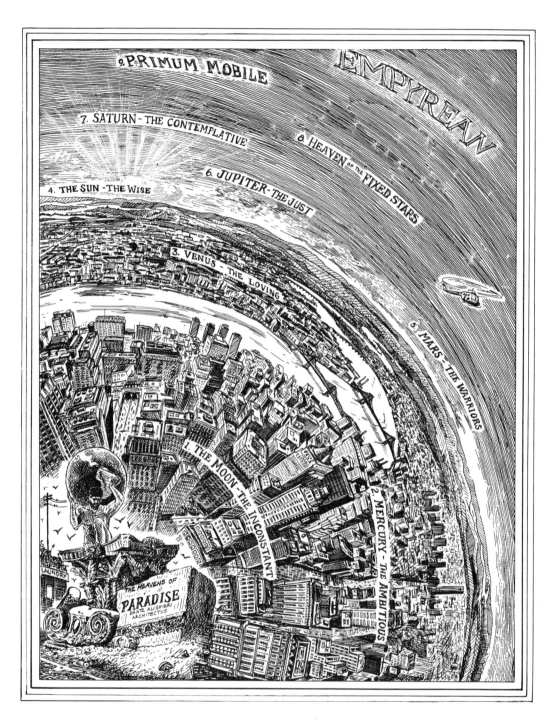

CANTO I, 3–6: THE HEAVENS OF PARADISE:
I've
been up in the dazzling bright of the highest
Heaven and I've seen things that anyone who
has been there either forgets or can't describe.

INTRODUCTION

THERE, TO THAT PREDESTINED PLACE, WE SOAR

By MICHAEL F. MEISTER, FSC, PhD.
Saint Mary's College of California

> *This is a man who from the deepest pit*
> *of all the universe up to this height*
> *has witnessed, one by one, the lives of souls,*
>
> *who begs you that you grant him through your grace*
> *the power to raise his vision higher still*
> *to penetrate the final blessedness.*
>
> *And I who never burned for my own vision*
> *more than I burn for his, with all my prayers*
> *I pray you—and I pray they are enough—*
>
> *that you through your own prayers dispel the mist*
> *of his mortality, that he may have*
> *the Sum of joy revealed before his eyes.*
>
> *I pray you also, Queen who can achieve*
> *your every wish, keep his affections sound*
> *once he has had the vision and returns.*
>
> PARADISO XXXIII: 22–36, MUSA

It is profoundly fitting that Dante afford St. Bernard, his final guide, the privilege of addressing the Virgin Mary on his behalf. As the mother of the Savior, she is the woman *par excellence* and Bernard is her greatest advocate. But in Christian theology she is, herself, the great advocate for us and in his words Bernard crowns the entire poem yet modestly frames the scope of Dante's *Commedia* as he would have it: in heartfelt prayer and visionary poetry. At once, we are prepared for the climax of the *Paradiso*—nothing less than the Beatific Vision itself.

Love, light, and vision are among the chief motifs that distribute the grace of Dante's *Paradiso*, this third and final canticle of his *Divina Commedia*. This grace passes from the poet and his poem to the reader and back again in a continual movement of wonder, astonishment, and veneration. While the entire *Commedia* is a grand act of faith in poetic form, it is here in the *Paradiso* where Dante's faith reaches toward the very being of God and brings us to the blinding vision of such Goodness that even poetry can only approach it obliquely. If grace is evidence of the beneficence of God, our poet—under the divine influence—creates here a celestial cathedral where we not only witness, but also participate in, the sublime worship of the angels and the saints.

Throughout the poem, Dante the poet is not satisfied that Dante the man (or we the reader, for that matter) simply "see" the sights he writes about. Were this the case, his comedy would lack something so elemental that it could well have stayed behind as a historical "period piece" of Italian literature—unique, perhaps, because it wasn't written in Latin.

Instead, he insists on the direct participation of both of us—pilgrim and reader—and in so doing, the experience of the poem becomes "virtual"—long before the word came to express modern visual reality. In this sense, the word becomes flesh—an incarnation with all its theological freight—here in poetry.

Several times, from the dizzying summits of Paradise, Beatrice asks Dante to look down to see how far he's come. This is not intended to give him, or us, mere cosmic reference points, though Dante leaves a trail of astronomical markers throughout the poem. Rather, it reminds him of where he has been and thus of what he has seen, experienced, and learned along the way. Moreover, in a curious fashion this "looking back" is an act that empowers the faith that has brought us here as readers: faith in Dante the poet, and faith (he hopes) in the God he writes into his poem. This faith moves us beyond mere seeing to become witnesses—itself evidence of our heightened participation in the poem's meaning.

If we have traveled with Dante from the "dark wood" of error to these supernal heights of light we are, like all pilgrims, made new in a mysterious way by the journey itself. But like all pilgrims, we must first estimate the cost of the venture. Does the mystery of transformation portended and the risks in undertaking it make it worthy of the ultimate risk—death? Dante may not have realized at the outset how lost he really was, and that he would have died so many times along the way to being found. Nor did he realize the extent to which he would participate in his own redemption. But for such a resurrection, Dante! For all his frights, his cries, his swoons in the *Inferno*, and his penitence and shame in the *Purgatorio*, here in the *Paradiso* he begins to comprehend for the first time, perhaps, the ultimate unity of existence, its final purpose, and its driving force.

Striving—instinctively—to escape the moral crisis he faced at the beginning of the *Inferno*, Dante was forced to reassess the broad scope of his life. Virgil made it unmistakably clear to him that the only way up was down. Even here, from the crown of the cosmos, we cannot—we must not—forget the cavity of revulsion that is the eternal home of the evil one. The horrors of the Hell he narrates are fearsome, coarse, and often overwhelming. Imaginative genius aside, the tragedy of eternal damnation is made all the more poignant when Dante's encounters bring him face to face with friends, relatives, and others made famous by their own infamies.

At the same time, the *Paradiso* would be shallow without the two previous canticles. Dante moves, often by virtue of his own curiosity, from poet to character. And this tidal motion throughout the poem almost literally carries us away from the safety of our ports and onto the sea. Much like Ulysses in *Inferno* XXVI, he urges us—his comrades—to shun the ordinary life and embark with him on a "mad flight" that will end, this time not with destruction, but here where we will see God.

But once Dante—the man—has climbed along the grizzled shanks of Satan himself, the ultimate horror gives way to blessed hope. The mountain prefigured so early in the poem reappears, and the upward thrust of the *Commedia* combines spiritually with Dante's purgation so that we now find ourselves rising effortlessly from the Garden of Earthly Delight into the Ptolomean cosmos—quaint and elegant to post-Hubble humans.

The climb *up* the Mount of Purgatory is as it says. The man Dante's ever-present confusion and soulful disarray seem shared by all the spirits he first meets there. *They* have *really* died! Has he, yet? Amazed as they are at his solidity, is this what must finally become permeable to the Divine Light so that he—and we—can become truly *animated*? Is Paradise for Dante not so much the ability to *see* the Light as to become the Light?

And so, Beatrice initiates him into the mysteries of the heavenly realms and through-out redirects his love toward the Ultimate until he, like her, is able to contemplate the utter fullness of Love Itself. As the Light of God becomes more apparent, the more they (and we) are drawn upward toward that eternal Flame that lightens the spirit, delights the heart, and enlightens the soul. Dante's continual use of visual imagery as a point of reference powerfully reinforces not only what can be seen, but also what *must* be seen—within.

An act of contemplation, a grand meditation on the true Kingdom of God, and illuminated by His very Light, the *Paradiso*'s ever upward motion is also a means Dante uses to communicate that it stands beyond the reach of time. We who are accustomed to think in terms of light-years can still savor the frisson when in Canto XXII Beatrice proposes that Dante look down on how far they'd come. Speed and distance now contrast with earlier gravity and effort.

Nowhere is this contrast between realms more apparent than when we consider the true horror of Hell as a forever in time. Heaven: a place of Ultimate peace, of music, joy, and praise beyond telling, of sights beyond seeing—this is what he wants us to consider. How often here does Beatrice smile? And when she does, her radiance increases so that the Light of God becomes more manifest. Is the Beatific Vision a Smile? And does that Smile embrace all of creation in an affirmation of its goodness and its ultimate goal? Dante would know and have us know in spite of the danger!

Using his image of the heavenly Rose, the *Paradiso*, like the two earlier canticles, "blossoms" for Dante and his readers through a series of ongoing questions. He is a superb enquirer. "How can this be?" he asks again and again. Does he go too far at times? Yes:

> *Yet even heaven's most illumined soul*
> *that Seraph who sees God with keenest eye,*
> *could not explain what you have asked to know.*

> *The truth you seek to fathom lies so deep*
> *in the abyss of the eternal law,*
> *it is cut off from every creature's sight.*
>
> (PARADISO XXI: 91–96, MUSA)

But his questions not only effect our "growth," they also act as a great compass and together we learn and we navigate the poetic universe he creates as his guides and interlocutors answer and direct him onward.

While the contemplation of God's Kingdom is serious, there is at the same time a certain playfulness in his mystical familiarity with this place. He often addresses us directly, and in so doing, puts out his hand and brings us alongside the action.

But the questioner is also questioned. The plan of the *Commedia* includes numerous "boundaries" or "stops" beyond which he cannot immediately proceed. These range throughout each of the three canticles and, among others, mark experiences of great emotion, moments of growth, and points of progress. And so, late in the *Paradiso*, Dante undergoes the Great Examination. At Canto XXIV, on the verge of Heaven proper, Beatrice stops to address the saints so radiantly displayed before them. Soon three Apostles come forth to question the traveler before he can proceed. Travelers from time immemorial have been challenged along their journeys, and Dante is no exception. Here he brings us to that ultimate catechism, beyond which is the Sight he has longed for all his lifetime.

Saints Peter, James, and John frequently kept the closest company with Jesus and were witness to his greatest miracles. Knowing his Bible, Dante was also well versed in the theological teachings expounded by Aquinas, so that this "trinity" comprises an appropriate panel of judges before whom all souls bound for Heaven come on "matters of state." What are these matters? Faith, Hope, and Love—quite simply. One does not enter upon the sight of Sight Itself without the "trinity" of these virtues stamped into one's passport. Only by grace are they given, and so it is now that the "grace" of the poem becomes the grace by which its poet enters the very vision it betokens.

In the ritual of university examination, Dante prepares himself to propound in the language of philosophic eloquence the true significance of these theological virtues. From the beginning of the *Commedia* Beatrice has also been a grace; she was such throughout Dante's life. She who set the journey of the poem in motion now stands—reflecting toward him the radiance of the Divine Effulgence—as he replies to the Apostles' questions.

The examination covers three cantos, and while the sophistication of the dialogue is impressive—not to mention its spectacular setting—we should not be distracted from Dante's utter sincerity. Faith sustained him as a Christian believer; hope infused his vision of the world around him and enabled him to continue in the face of so many disappointments; love led him to the poem we read. It is both clever and fascinating that Dante's curiosity about St. John leads him to stare so intensely that he is blinded during his examination on Love. Not only is this a wonderful effect, it also forces Dante to speak about love directly from his soul and thereby navigate precisely between lesser loves that have distracted him on his journey toward the true Love that beckons just beyond his sight. It is also quite fascinating here that St. John does not ask Dante to *define* love. Mirroring Dante's curiosity, he seems more interested in *what* Dante loves and *whom*. In the end, the pilgrim's "vision" is restored to him in such a way that he will see right into Heaven. All this by Beatrice's gaze, as though to exemplify what he knew from the theology of his time—that seeing leads to love.

At such a point as this, with a final look downward upon the universe below, his poetic force gathers boldly and quickly toward its climax. The vision of God may be as intimate as what we look for in each other, or be conceived as broadly scattered in the creation we see limitlessly behind and before us. We are all, to an extent, gifted with the hope of what Dante says he saw. It is for each of us to reach for that vision—more than that, it is our destiny to attain it. That we can rub shoulders here with one whose discernment is so sweeping that even poetry fails is, hopefully, to experience in a veiled way what the life we have been given is for.

Dante's vision incarnated for him—*inworded*—truly what he believed about the afterlife. But this vision was also *enfleshed* by him in his native language, and populated far and wide with natives who embodied the moral continuum of his time. At this end of his poem, he has come a lifetime and a universe from the "dark wood" of the *Inferno* to the Amphitheatre of the Rose. He is surrounded.

And this, perhaps, leads us to consider the architectural signification of his story, because it is, to a great extent, dependent on circles. Whether we think of them as "rounds," "levels," or "spheres," the *Commedia* sets out to encompass every extent of our imagination—and it has succeeded for 700 years!

In the *Inferno,* the circles get smaller; in the *Paradiso* they get larger. In the *Inferno,* there is nothing left to embrace, all hope must be abandoned. But in the *Paradiso* there is everything—it is beyond our fondest hopes. And this is what Dante's pilgrimage has brought him to see. He has come from emptiness to substance; a desperate, lonely man to one who keeps company with Saints. The end of his poem is very much like a death. It collapses, it can no longer see, it ceases to speak. In striving to square the circle Dante the poet has attempted the impossible. But in so doing, Dante the man has found the numinous love that moves the sun and all the stars. Would that such a discovery embolden any one of us to live to attempt every outrageous feat!

Laudate

Reading has such power that it enables us to enter a world created by another. It sparks the imagination, it enriches our vocabulary, and it confers new being upon us. Reading Dante is not necessarily recreation, but like all great literature, it has the ability to re-create us and make us new. Furthermore, some great works of art stand out as beacons of the human spirit and mark life itself with their radiance. This luminance is not fleeting, but endures every time the work is taken up. A painting is seen again and again, a piece of music played, a drama performed, and a book . . . . Such a book!

With this publication of the *Paradiso,* the daring and contemporary "trilogy" of Sanders and Birk—itself a vision in word and illustration—now comes to a conclusion and brings the whole of Dante's sweeping poem into the twenty-first century. Their production offers the readers of Dante an unmistakable experience of the living essence of this 700-year-old poem, enabling a dialogue with Dante and his world that he himself might not have dreamed. This kind of dialogue leads to new levels of meaning and understanding, especially when our openness is accompanied by the vibrant text and captivating images that will reward the reader who here embarks on the last great segment of Dante's amazing vision of Heaven.

Skillfully comingling the long tradition of translating and adapting the *Divina Commedia* with an equally abundant tradition of visually illustrating pivotal points in the text, this present work of Sanders and Birk enables yet another generation of readers to encounter the living presence of Dante much as he himself encountered the numerous individuals who populate his sublime poem. The fresh and unpretentious approach of this new version invites readers to (re-)discover Dante the man and his world, Dante the poet, and Dante the chief character of his poem. Together, they engage us on a journey with cosmic dimensions and everlasting implications.

On several levels, the *Commedia* of Dante is extremely visual. The sustained and distinct structure of his meter over more than 14,000 lines causes us to "look at" the poem in awe. At the same time, his constant validation of what he sees by referring it to our "ordinary" experience disarms us and draws us into the "real" vision that unfolds canto by canto until the poem can no longer sustain itself in words. A point of failure? Hardly! Here is where the near infinite richness of the artistic tradition comes into play. Each of the numerous editions and translations of his poem over the centuries represents a new stake in life and in the future. The poem lives not only on its own, but like all of us, by virtue of those who sustain us.

When Sanders and Birk took up this project with their now widely known *Inferno*, they themselves embarked on a pilgrimage that had all the trappings of hazard and adventure. But throughout they have sought—by virtue of their collaboration and their unique gifts—to sustain Dante, not as a fragile ghost from the Middle Ages, but as a man with a bold vision. Like all who have brought Dante to word and to sight since then, their goal has been to make him accessible, to open doors, to break down barriers. They are hardly warriors, but they *are* intrepid and venturesome. What they (and we) discover by virtue of their efforts is that Dante's vision still addresses us from out of the past and that he is versatile enough to make that vision clear to us in the unabashed argot of a twenty-first century world he might have imagined only in a poem. Birk's illustrations cogently mingle "this world" with the "other world" of the poem so that the effect of the overall work is all the more engaging. Both artists have, in their unique way, mined for us the fortune of the past and brought the abundance of Dante's poem to bear in a new light. Bringing the poem's immense patrimony within our reach, their achievement adds to its richness and ours and brings us tangibly closer to the serious danger of being changed by what we see and what we read.

CANTO I

ARGUMENT

In the opening lines of the third canticle of the Divine Comedy, *Dante states that he's been to Heaven and back and that he will do his best to describe the amazing things he saw there as well as he can remember them. He explains that the experience of Paradise is way beyond human comprehension, and he calls on the inspiration of Apollo and the Muses to help him write, and hopes that his* Commedia *may inspire others. Standing in the Garden of Eden and having just drunk from the stream of Good Memories, the Lethe, Dante notices that Beatrice is staring directly into the Sun. He follows her gaze but can't stand the glare, and so turns to look at her instead. As he does, he has the sensation that they're rising, floating up into the sky. Dante hears music and finds himself inside a misty glow of light as if in a fog. Beatrice explains that they are indeed rising, and goes on to explain the laws of universal gravity.*

The glory of God is everywhere and shines in
all things, flowing through the universe, glowing
stronger in some places and less in others. I've
been up in the dazzling bright of the highest
Heaven and I've seen things that anyone who   5
has been there either forgets or can't describe.
Think: the closer we get to that desired
height, our brains sink into depths so deep
that our memories can't find their way back up
again. But now I'm going to do my best to   10
share the bits of Heaven's kingdom that I can
remember and turn them into this poem.

Apollo, I'm calling on your help to finish off this part.
I'm going to need your inspiration if I'm ever going
to deserve to wear your laurel crown. So far I've   15
only been asking the Muses up on Mt. Parnassus
to help me write this thing, but I'm gonna need
your help to write about Heaven's arena.
I'll need your music to flow through me, like
when Johnny won the golden fiddle in that   20
Devil Went Down to Georgia country-western song.

If you'd help me out even just a little bit,
maybe my descriptions can be more than just
a mere shadow of the amazing stuff that's
burning in my head right now. And then maybe   25
I'll be worthy enough to stand under the poets'
tree, deserving of its laurels—the crown that
you and my theme may help me deserve.

It's so rare that our leaders or poets ever
deserve that crown, because most men are   30
too scared and ashamed to even strive for it.
So when someone like me *does* reach out
and strive for the laurel wreath, it must really
make you happy. I know even one little match can
start a huge fire, and maybe after I get through   35
writing this thing, someone else will come
along and do a better job of it than I have.

Throughout the year the sun rises from different
places on the horizon, and at the vernal equinox
in spring, when the hours of daylight are equal
to night and the sun is in the constellation of Aries,
the world is warmed and fertile after the long winter.

It was March 21st, and just after noon over in
the Garden of Eden on the peak of Purgatory.
It would've been morning back in Europe then, and
Beatrice turned to her left and faced the north, looking
straight into the Sun and staring without blinking,
like she was wearing sunglasses or something.

And like the Sun reflecting off a windowpane,
or like a traveler heading toward home,
back the way he came, there was something
about the strength and intensity of her gaze
that fascinated me and made my eyes
follow hers, until I was staring at the Sun too.
The Garden of Eden was completely amazing—
all of my senses seemed way more intense and
heightened there than they ever were here on Earth.

I couldn't look at it too long, but I was able to
see that the Sun was surrounded by flames
and oozed like molten lava in the sky. And then
all of a sudden it got super-bright, like today was
shining down on tomorrow or something, or like
God had thrown in a second Sun just to spice things up.

Beatrice just stood there, staring into the eternal
fireball in the sky. I had to turn away and I looked
at her. As I watched her, I started to feel really odd.
I can't explain how it felt, but until you experience
it yourself you'll just have to try to imagine it as
best you can. Or maybe it'll help if you try to
think of Ovid's story of how Glaucus felt after
he ate the herb that turned him into a Sea God.
I think they call it "transhumanizing" or something.

CANTO I, 64–66: DANTE AND BEATRICE:

*Beatrice just stood there, staring into the eternal
fireball in the sky. I had to turn away and I looked
at her. As I watched her, I started to feel really odd.*

DANTE'S PARADISO

Dear God, I don't know if it was only my soul that
started to rise then, or if my body went along with it;
all I know is that it was Your light that carried me up.   75

The farthest reaches of Heaven spin in constant
yearning for You, and the beautiful music of their
Spheres colliding is Your creation, too. I was surrounded
by their amazing melodies as I rose, until I saw the
giant expanse of Heaven spread out and flamed with   80
the Sun's rays as far as I could see, stretched across
the sky like an ocean. The sight of it all laid out
in front of me gave me a rush and made me want
to learn more about it all than I ever had before.

Beatrice must have seen me spacing out,   85
because even before I started firing off questions
she spoke and tried to calm me down.

"You've filled your mind with foggy ideas about
what this place was *supposed* to look like,"
she said, "and now you're having trouble   90
seeing the reality that's right in front of you.
And don't think we're still on Earth. We've been
rising faster than a bullet up into Heaven now."

That put me a little more at ease, but as
soon as I was grasping what she'd said,   95
a whole new thought bubbled up in my head:

"You're right. That *is* what I was thinking," I said.
"But I also don't understand how I can be
rising through elements that are lighter than me."

She took a deep breath and looked at me   100
like a fourth grade teacher might look at a
hyperactive kid who missed a Ritalin dose.

"Everything in the universe has its rightful
place," she began, "It is all ordered
to reflect God. All rational beings—men,   105
women, angels—are able to discern this

grand pattern of Divine Excellence. And within
this whole system of order there is a hierarchy.

"All things—like rocks, bananas, sparrows,
and stuff—instinctively know their place in the   110
system according to how perfect—or imperfect—
they are. Everything in the universe moves to its
own place in the sea of being, and each of them
is guided to his destination by instinct. It is this
force that makes fire rise up and gravity pull   115
down, that fills humans with love and purpose.
It's what keeps the world from exploding. Instinct
is the strongest and most pure path to God, not
only among all the animals and nonliving things,
but also among humans who have brains and hearts.   120

"The bright light of Providence, which regulates
everything under the Sun and beyond, casts a
calming glow on even the farthest reaches of Heaven.
And all of us are flying toward our predestined place,
shot forward by the strength and power of God's   125
slingshot, which is always aimed toward Heaven.

"But just like sometimes a painting may not
come out exactly as an artist hoped it would
because maybe the materials were bad or something—
one of God's creatures, even armed with instinct and   130
good intentions, may in fact stray from the true path
simply because it has the power to do so. And
like how lightning in a storm seems almost like
it's pulled to the ground, man's impulse, once
it's been swayed, can be drawn to Earthly things.   135

"But in your case, you shouldn't be any
more amazed at flying up here than you
would be at water running downstream.
You don't weigh anything anymore, and
staying down there weightless would have   140
been as weird as a flame that doesn't flicker."

And then she turned and looked up to the Heavens.

CANTO II

ARGUMENT

Dante warns his readers that he is heading into a new realm with his story and he calls on the Muses to help him find the words to describe what happened. He and Beatrice rise up into the sky and are drawn into the First Heaven of the Moon, which seems foggy but bright to Dante. Ever curious, he asks Beatrice what causes the dark spots on the Moon you can see from Earth. Beatrice gives a long explanation in which she shoots his ideas down as unfounded. She then explains the nature of the radiances of the Heavens and the concept of the Empyrean Heaven and the Primum Mobile, and how the Celestial Intelligences pass through the various levels and glow from within.

If you've been paddling your little kayak along
behind my ship's flowing rhymes through the
waters of my travels so far, you might want to
turn back here before you lose sight of the shore.
Beware of the deep. It may be that if you   5
lost me now, you might lose yourself.

Now I set sail toward unknown seas.
Minerva, Goddess of Wisdom, fills my sails;
Apollo, God of Poetry, mans the helm; and
all nine Muses light the way toward the stars   10
of the Bear constellation. The few of you
reading this who have devoted your lives
to searching, yearning, for the bread of angels
in this life, let your boats follow mine into the
high seas. Follow in the wake that I churn as I   15
part the seas ahead of you. The Argonauts, who
sailed with Jason on his quest, were not as
amazed by what they saw as you will be.

Drawn by that unquenchable and endless
thirst for God's Kingdom, the two of us rose as   20
fast as human sight when it looks to the skies.
My eyes were on Beatrice. She looked to Heaven,
and as fast as an e-mail fires across the Internet
and lands on your buddy's computer screen, I found myself
in a place where wonder filled all my thoughts.   25

Then my girl turned toward me, since
she already knew that I had a ton of
questions before I had even said anything.
"Concentrate on God with gratitude," she said,
"He has now drawn us up to the Moon, His first star."   30

It seemed like we were inside a cloud or something,
but at the same time it seemed all
hard and bright, too, as if we were inside
a diamond, sparkling in the sun. That eternal
pearl of the Heavens embraced us, drew   35
us in, like water embraces sunlight.

CANTO II, 26–28: IN THE HEAVEN OF THE MOON:
*Then my girl turned toward me, since
she already knew that I had a ton of
questions before I had even said anything.*

On Earth it's impossible for us to imagine a
solid entering a solid, but that's what happened—
body entered body. And inside of me there now
burned the desire to see Jesus, that Being in whom we   40
can witness the union of God's Nature with our own.
Once this happens, we'll be able to see
everything we've believed to be true through our
faith alone until that time: that which is unprovable
but evident, the primal truths, incontrovertible.   45

"Believe me," I said to Beatrice, "Every ounce of
gratitude I have is to Him for having brought me up
here from the mortal world. But I was hoping, now
that we're here, that you could explain what makes
the dark spots that we can see on the Moon.   50
On Earth people have all kinds of theories."

"It shouldn't surprise you that human judgment
comes to false conclusions when it doesn't
have any clues provided by its senses," she
said, smiling. "After all, even when *all* the   55
senses are working the mind can still fall
short in its conclusions. But tell me,
what do *you* think might cause the spots?"

"I would guess that the differences we see from Earth
are caused by different densities in the Moon," I said.   60

"I can assure you that you'll soon realize
your beliefs are erroneous," she replied.
"Listen carefully and I'll explain why:

"The Eighth Sphere of Heaven is where the fixed
stars of the different constellations are located.   65
They shine with a wide range of both brilliance and
quantity. If this was caused by different densities,
as you suggest, that would mean that one property
or virtue would be distributed more or less equally
between them. But instead, they each show   70
different qualities, caused by different active
principles, which your theory would negate.

"What's more, if the dark areas on the Moon were
    caused by density alone, then the substance of this place
    we are now would be thin and translucent in some places   75
    and thicker in others, in the way a piece of meat has fatty parts
    and lean parts. Or the difference in thicknesses would have
    to go back and forth, the way that pages in a book alternate.

"Furthermore," she continued, "if that were true,
    then the Moon wouldn't completely block out the light   80
    of the Sun during an eclipse, since the light of the
    Sun would still show through the thin parts of the Moon.
    But it doesn't. So let's look at another example, and
    if I'm right, then I'll have shown your theory to be false.

"So, if differences in the substance of the   85
    Moon were the cause," she went on, "then
    that means that at some points it would have to be
    thicker. And these, therefore, would be places
    where the rays of the Sun would be reflected back,
    just like color is reflected off a mirrored surface.   90

"Now, sticking with your theory you might argue
    that even with reflection it might be that the rays
    are dimmer in some places since they reflect
    through a thicker substance. But a simple experiment,
    the process by which men usually support their   95
    conjectures, will show that this is not the case:

"Take two mirrors and place them out in front of
    you at the same distance, spread apart from each
    other. Then take a third mirror and place it between
    them, but even farther away. Now, if you stand facing   100
    the three of them with a light behind you so that the
    mirrors reflect it back at you, you'll see that even
    though the image in the mirror farthest away looks
    smaller than in the other two, the light will still be
    reflected back as bright as in the closer ones.   105

"So," she said, continuing methodically,
"in hopes that your errors will melt away
    from where they're frozen in your brain
    like ice cubes in a cocktail glass, let me

explain a concept so new to you it's like
light so living it trembles in your sight.

"You see, in the Empyrean Heaven of godly peace
spins the Primum Mobile, the Ninth Heaven,
which is surrounded by the Empyrean Heaven,
and which receives from it a power that it then
transmits unaltered to the next Sphere. The
Eighth Heaven, also called the Heaven of
the Fixed Stars, receives the power and
distributes it to the different stars within its
Sphere. The seven Heavens below each
modify the power received from above
so that they can use it for their proper
goals and to influence things on Earth.

"Now pay attention to how I rationally explain
the phenomenon of the lunar spots so that you
will be able to understand it on your own,"
she continued. "The power and the motion of
the Heavens is necessarily controlled by the
Celestial Intelligences, just as the mechanic
moves the wrench in the mysteries of auto repair.
And so, from these Intelligences, or the angelic order,
if you prefer, the Heaven of the Fixed Stars contains
the knowledge and purposes of them. And just as
the soul within the dust of your body is shared by
the different organs inside of you, each one designed
for a different purpose, so does that Celestial Intelligence
pass through and expand through the different
Heavens even though it spins in unity around itself.

"Each star receives and is inspired by a different power
and forms a different compound," she expounded, "sort of
like how your soul inspires the form of your body with life.
Since the source of the power of the Angelic Intelligences
is God, that power expresses itself as radiant light, like the
gleam in a human eye. It's from this, and not from the differences
in thickness or thinness of materials, that you see the differences
in the light of the Moon. Each has unique properties and therefore
each shines with a particular quality of light. This is the principle
that produces dark and bright, each according to its worth."

110

115

120

125

130

135

140

145

CANTO III

ARGUMENT

A group of faces appears indistinctly in the fog of the First Sphere of Paradise, the Moon. They are the souls of those who were wavering or inconsistent in their commitment to God while alive. Dante meets Piccarda dei Donati, a nun who was abducted from her convent and forced into a long marriage. She explains that all the souls in the First Sphere are happy just to be in Paradise, even if their station is the lowest. She points out the Empress Constance, the mother of Frederick II of Sicily, who was also forced to leave her life as a nun for marriage. The souls sing the hymn "Ave Maria" and fade into the fog, and Dante turns to Beatrice only to see that she is glowing with a radiance that stuns him so much that he forgets what he wanted to ask her next.

I was just a kid when I first fell in love with
Beatrice, all tongue-tied and heartsick;
and now, decades later, she had revealed
to me the beauty of logic and description.
As she finished explaining about the Moon   5
I lifted my head to admit my ignorance to her,
when suddenly a vision appeared in front
of me, and it freaked me out so much
that I forgot what I was going to say.

The vision was faint, like when you see your   10
face in a car window as you're walking by,
or the reflections in a clear, shallow puddle,
where you can still see the sidewalk underneath.
And it was pale, too, as hard to make out as
a white napkin on a white tablecloth.   15

It was amazing. I saw a huge crowd of faces that
looked like they were all dying to say something.
At first I thought they were just reflections—
making the opposite mistake of Narcissus
when he saw himself in the pool of water—   20
and I turned to look behind me, but there
was no one there. When I turned back
again, I saw Beatrice in a glow of light, her
eyes all twinkling as she grinned at me.

"You shouldn't be surprised to see me   25
smile when you doubt what you're seeing
with your own eyes," she said. "Trust what
you can see and don't look for things you can't.
These forms are completely real, and they are
here because they each somehow broke a   30
promise to God. You should talk to them and
trust what they say. Now they are peaceful and
brimming over with the truth of God's light."

I turned toward the ghost who seemed most
keen to speak, and suddenly I had this crazy   35
surge of desire that made me insecure.

"Dear soul, basking here in the endless
  light of God and sipping on the juice of
  immortality that can never really be known
  until it's tasted, I'd be ecstatic if you were   40
  kind enough to take just a minute and tell
  me who you are and what happened to you."

"I'd be more than happy to," she replied, glowing.
  "I can no more reject a fair request than ignore
  the love of God himself, which blankets His   45
  kingdom. Back on Earth, I was a virgin nun;
  I'd bet if you thought for a while you'd remember
  who I was—though to be honest, I'm way
  better looking these days. My name is Piccarda,
  and I'm here with all these other blessed   50
  souls happily plodding along within the
  lowest Sphere of Paradise. We're thrilled
  with our place in the Divine Order that He
  has set for us, even though this first Sphere
  of the Moon is farthest from God, and slowest,   55
  too, and we're all here because we somehow
  failed to come good on our promises to God."

"Oh yeah," I replied. "At first I didn't recognize
  you, the way you're all glowing and radiant up
  here. You look a lot different than you did back on   60
  Earth, so I had a hard time remembering just who
  you are until you'd explained it. Now I can picture
  what you used to look like. But I'm curious about
  something: All you guys seem totally happy
  and content up here, but ... don't you want to   65
  move up in Heaven and be closer to God?"

She smiled at me along with all those other happy
  ghosts, and her explanation was so full of joy it
  was as if she was falling in love for the first time.

"Dear Brother," she said, "It is the strength   70
  and honesty of our love that keeps our
  will in check. Or more simply, we don't

CANTO III, 47–49: PICCARDA:

> *"I'd bet if you thought for a while you'd remember
> who I was—though to be honest, I'm way
> better looking these days. My name is Piccarda."*

want what we can't have, and what we have
is all that we want. Any desire for a higher
place would not correspond with God's will,   75
which is that we all be here where we are
now. If you think for a second about the
nature of love, then you'll see that it's
impossible for conflict to exist here.

"The purpose of Paradise is to be here within   80
His will, and we all know that there is no
other will than God's. Our place in the
order of His Heavenly Spheres pleases us
as much as it pleases God Himself. We all
find our peace and fulfillment in His desire,   85
which is the sea toward which all created
beings in the universe swim together."

Then it really hit home: everywhere
in Heaven is actually Paradise, even
though God's light doesn't necessarily   90
shine on everyone equally. But you know
how sometimes you can get your fill of
Mexican food but still be hungry for sushi?
That's how I felt after Piccarda explained Heaven—
but I still wanted her to finish telling the story   95
of her life and how she ended up here.

"I've always been inspired by the perfect,
virtuous life of Saint Clare of Assisi, who is
now in a Sphere up above," Piccarda explained.
"She founded a Franciscan Order for nuns   100
whose only desire in life is to wake each
morning and sleep each night as a bride of
Christ, who accepts all vows of love. When I
was young I turned from the vain world to wear
the habit and follow her teaching, dedicating my   105
life to her. But I was stolen, violently, from the
convent by wicked men and taken away, and only
God knows what happened to my life after that.

"This glowing soul you see on my right,
shining with the light of the Moon, knows   110
firsthand what I'm talking about. She was a
nun, too, but her veil was torn from her against
her will and her vows. But even while she
was forced to live in the world as a wife,
against her sacred promises, she kept   115
the ideals of the veil closed tightly over
her heart. She is the vivid ghost of the
Empress Constance, who was wed to
Henry VI of Germany and whose son was
Frederick II, the last Roman Emperor."   120

And with that she began to sing *Ave Maria*,
and slowly drifted away from me like
a penny dropped down a wishing well.
I watched her go until I couldn't
see her anymore, and then turned   125
back to face my Beatrice, my desire.
I was confused and full of doubts, but
she seemed to glow with a brightness
so intense that I could barely look at her,
and it made me hold off on my questions.   130

CANTO IV

ARGUMENT

Listening to Piccarda has got Dante wondering about two things: first, if both she and Constance were forced away from their vows, how can that be held against them—and why are they less deserving of blessedness? Second, since Piccarda talked about the Moon being her allotted place in Heaven, does that mean that Plato's ideas about the soul's relationship to the stars was right after all? Beatrice explains to him that everyone in Paradise floats in the Empyrean, but that they appear to Dante here so that he can comprehend their position better in his mortal mind. She also explains the difference between what we want to do and what we consent to do under pressure or fear—this clears up his doubts about justice in Heaven being unfair. But Dante has another question: is it possible for someone to do good things to make up for vows that they haven't fulfilled?

If you were to put two equally tasty plates of food
on either side of a hungry man, he might starve before
he could choose between them. The same man, trapped
between two fires of equal intensity, might stand paralyzed
in fear before he could decide which way to run; just as a   5
dog would sit trembling, immobile, between two dog biscuits.

So I guess I shouldn't blame or congratulate
myself when I stood there confused, pondering
two doubts so long that I remained silent out
of necessity. I didn't say anything, but my   10
expression must have shown my questions
more clearly than anything I could have said.

And as easily as Daniel read and interpreted the
dreams of Nebuchadnezzar and managed to calm
him down a bit, Beatrice did the same to me.   15

"I can tell by looking at you that you're so worked up
about two different things that you can't even get
a word out," she said. "On the one hand you're
wondering why, if somebody's desire to do good
is strong enough, how can somebody else's use   20
of force against them cause their worthiness to be
judged any less? And at the same time you're pondering
another idea, wondering if Plato was right when he thought
that each person's soul returns to its star after death.

"Both of these questions are bothering your   25
conscience equally. Let me, therefore, deal
first with the second, more insidious, one.

"To start with, no one, not the most pious
angel, not Moses, Samuel, either of the
Johns—not even Mary herself—has a place   30
in any other Heaven than the souls you just met;
nor is their blessedness any more or less eternal.
All of them reside in the Empyrean, and
all of them have it good—though some of
them sense the Eternal Spirit more than others.   35

CANTO IV, 8–10: DANTE'S MEDITATIONS:
*I stood there confused, pondering
two doubts so long that I remained silent out
of necessity.*

"The ones you saw appeared to you here in
this level only so that you could grasp
that their place in the Empyrean is lowest,
not because they actually reside here. Since
you're still human, you understand things   40
through your senses, and seeing them
here makes it easier for you to understand.
That's the same reason why in the Bible they
use human descriptions, saying that God has
hands and feet, for instance, but actually they're   45
just metaphors. It's also why the three archangels—
Gabriel, Michael, and Raphael—are
portrayed as humans by the Church.

"If what Plato says about souls and Heaven
in his book *Timaeus* is meant to be taken   50
literally, then what you just saw contradicts
him," she explained. "He wrote that the soul
returns to its own star. He believes it was
separated when it took physical form.

"Now maybe he didn't mean for us to take   55
him literally, in which case he was making
an admirable point. If what he really meant
was that the stars have influence over the
course of people's lives, then he's got some
good ideas there. This is a concept that's   60
been misunderstood for a long time, with
the result that people have named the
planets things like Jupiter, Mercury, and Mars.

"The other question that's bugging you
isn't as dangerous," she continued,   65
"because not even all its errors could drag
you away from me. To mortal eyes, our
system of justice seems unfair. This fact
should reinforce one's faith, rather than fuel
one's doubts. But since the answer is not   70
beyond your power of comprehension,
I'll explain it to you so you can relax a bit.

"Now then," she began, "if one suffers
violence but doesn't do anything to contribute
to it, they still can't be excused, because one's   75
will to resist can never be beaten. The will is
like a flame that will burn skyward despite any
attempts to keep it from rising. So if one yields
to violence, even a little bit, it has assisted
force, and that's what the souls you saw did.   80

"After all, they could have gone back to their
convents, right? If they had kept their will—
like St. Lawrence or Mucius did in their fires—
then they would have returned, once
they were free, back to the pious lives   85
they had been dragged away from.
But strength of will that strong is rare.

"Now, if you've followed my discussion, you
can discard the thought that was bothering
you, that of the apparent injustice of God.   90
But I can tell that there's something else
that's still holding you up, and you'll wear
yourself out trying to solve it alone.

"Earlier," she went on, "I told you that
souls in Heaven can't lie since they're so   95
close to the Primal Truth. But then Piccarda
went and said that Constance never gave up
her devotion to the veil, and in your mind
that seems to contradict what I said.

"Look: a lot of times people will do things that   100
they normally would hate if they are driven by fear.
If you remember the story of Alcmaeon, which you
saw carved into the walls of Purgatory, you'll recall
how he killed his own mother out of a sense
of fear and obligation to his father's dying wish.   105
So you can see how, in some circumstances,
will and violence mix to cause actions that
cannot be excused. Absolute will does not

agree with sin, but when it fears that
resistance will hurt it worse, it often gives in.   110
So you can see now that Piccarda was talking
about the absolute will back there, and I'm
talking about the relative will. So you see,"
she concluded, "we're both telling the truth."

And with that rippling stream from   115
the fountain of holy truth, my nagging
questions were answered.

"You who are loved by the First Lover,"
I said, overcome, "how can I ever show
you how deeply grateful I am for your   120
words? They wash over me and warm my
insides with a sense of new life. I can never
thank you enough, but I pray that the Big Guy
will repay you somehow. Now I understand
that we can never really be satisfied in   125
our minds until we hear the real Truth.

"Once you discover the Truth your thoughts
are finally able to rest in your head like
a puppy in its basket. And they have to
rest sooner or later, or else all hope is   130
pointless. Doubts seem to spring up like
weeds under the feet of truth, and all that
does is keep my thoughts in the clouds.
And this new realization gives me the
confidence to ask, respectfully, one more   135
thing that is still bugging me: Is there
anything that somebody can do to make
up for unfulfilled vows in their life?"

Beatrice looked straight at me then, and her
eyes were so beautiful and sparkling and so full   140
of the divine light that I couldn't return her gaze.
With my eyes turned down, I felt as if I might faint.

CANTO V

ARGUMENT

Beatrice explains the aspects of Free Will to Dante, how it's both God's greatest gift to man, and man's greatest gift back to God. Free Will is man's most important trait, she says, and explains the two aspects of a sacred vow: the pact with God, and the thing that is promised as sacrifice. The thing can be exchanged if it's approved by the Church and only if it is for something of equal or greater value. Beatrice emphasizes that it's important for all mankind to both keep vows and to make intelligent choices. Afterward, the two ascend into Mercury, the Second Sphere of Paradise, where Dante sees all kinds of lights and, at Beatrice's encouragement, speaks to one of them.

"**Y**ou shouldn't be so surprised that I
glow more brightly here," Beatrice said,
"or that your eyes can stand to look at me.
You see, the more one approaches perfection
above, the more one becomes perfect himself.   5
I can even see it in you. Your thoughts are
glowing full of His light, and once you've seen
it, that light will continue to inspire love. Even
if something less holy seduces a man to love,
it is still a reflected form of His light shining   10
through the other thing—though less perfectly.
And I know what you're thinking," she smiled.
"How is it possible to make amends with
God, you're wondering, if, for some reason,
you had to break a vow you made to Him?"   15

Beatrice wasted no time in starting
off Canto V with this whole spiel, and
almost in the same breath, went on:

"As giving as He is, the best gift God
ever created is the one that is most like   20
Him, the gift that He holds closest to His heart:
the freedom of the will. All of his creations
that possess an intellect—and no others—
are given it. So you can see how sacred a
vow to God is, since you're exercising your   25
Free Will to make it, and it depends on His
having allowed you that choice. So when man
and God seal this exchange of Free Will, man is
actually giving God's gift back to Him—and he's
giving it of his own Free Will, in perfect balance. So 30
how would it be possible to fix things if you mess up?
How could you use the Free Will you'd already given away?
That'd be stealing, and no good can come from that.

"So far, the main gist of what I'm talking
about should be pretty obvious to you,"   35
she said. "But since the Church grants
forgiveness through dispensations, that

seems to contradict what I just said. But sit
there a little and try to absorb what I've been saying—
it's a tough meal and isn't immediately digested.   40
Open your mind up to what I'm telling you,
or else it'll just go in one ear and out the other.

"There are two things that matter when one
makes a vow: there's the pledge of something,
and there's the contract of the promise. This   45
contract can't ever be canceled out until the
vow is completed. That's what I was talking
to you about earlier. The thing that's promised,
which can be exchanged by something else,
but only if a priest says it's OK—they're the   50
ones that can decide if the person's fit enough
to be absolved, and the ones with the power
to do the absolving. Or, as you know, the
Jews must make ritual sacrifices; but under
certain circumstances the offerings can be   55
changed. But no one should shift their
promises by themselves, and if a vow is
switched, the new thing has to be at least
as great if not bigger than the original thing,
or it's just a joke, right? And of course there   60
are certain sacred promises and vows that
are well beyond any other, and these acts
can never be substituted with anything else.

"No one should take a sacred promise lightly.
But by all means, don't make some crazy oath like   65
Jephthah did! He promised God he'd sacrifice the
first person to come out of his house if God let him
win the battle. He should've admitted his mistake
and it would've saved his daughter. Or like
Agamemnon, who killed his daughter, Iphigenia,   70
just to gain favorable winds for his ships. The story of
his rash decision has bummed people out for ages.

"So you see," she concluded, "as Christians,
you have to be careful about hasty promises.

Don't be as fickle as smoke in the wind, or   75
think that holy water's going to steam clean your
sins away. You've got the Old and New Testaments
to guide you, and the Pope, too. That is all
you should need to save your soul. If you're
ever tempted off the right path, then you should   80
stand up to it or else any Jew can point a finger
at you in contempt. Don't be like a runaway kid
who turns away from his own family, too proud
or ashamed to ask for help until it's too late."

What I've written here is exactly what Beatrice   85
said. And then, full of longing, she turned
and looked up to where all light is born.

She went completely still, and the change
in her made me step back a bit and hold
off on the other questions I had in my head.   90
And then, like an express elevator to the top
of a skyscraper, we rose up into Mercury, the
Second Sphere of Paradise. As we rose, she
seemed to get happier and happier, wrapped
in a swirling light that burned brighter as we   95
went, lighting up the whole place. And if she
could change a whole planet just by being
there, what do you think happened to me,
who's always been pretty moody to start with?

If you toss something into a calm pond,   100
all the fish will swim toward the splash,
thinking it might be something to eat.
It was like that when we got to Mercury.
A whole swarm of souls started toward us,
singing, *"One more to increase our love."*   105

And as they surrounded us I could
practically see their happiness
shining in their clear, bright glow.

CANTO V, 121–123: IN THE HEAVEN OF MERCURY:
Beatrice smiled and elbowed me
in the ribs. "Don't be scared," she said.
"Speak to them. . . ."

Just think how you'd feel if I stopped
my story right here, Reader. Wouldn't   110
you be dying to hear what happened next?
Then you can understand how I felt,
all keen to find out everything about
these new guys all around us.

"You must've been born into bliss," one   115
of them said to me, "since God has allowed
you to see this place before you've passed
away. Welcome. God's light illuminates all
of Paradise and all of us as well. If we
can be of service to you, feel free to ask."   120

Beatrice smiled and elbowed me
in the ribs. "Don't be scared," she said.
"Speak to them as if they were gods."

"Well," I began, "I see you in front of me in a bubble
of your own light, beaming from your eyes and   125
exploding with rays when you smile. But I have no
idea who you are, my friend, or why your place is
here in this glowing Sphere of Mercury, a planet
that's often hidden from the Earth by the Sun's rays."

And as I spoke I could see that   130
ball of light flare up in front of me,
brighter than it had been before.

You know how the Sun seems to
gather around itself on foggy days,
glowing through the mist? That's   135
kind of like what he looked like. That
soul glowed with its own light,
overflowing with happiness.

I'll tell you what he said in the next canto.

CANTO VI

ARGUMENT

Still in the Second Heaven, the Sphere of Mercury, the speaker introduces himself as Justinian, former Emperor of Rome, who devoted himself to codifying Roman Law after he was converted by Bishop Agapetus. He then goes off on a long speech about the history of the Roman Empire and the deeds of various Caesars. He bags on the Guelfs and the Ghibellines, and he explains that the souls around him in that Sphere of Paradise are those who acted for good causes but also out of their own desires for personal fame. Finally, he goes on about the good deeds and sad ending of one of the souls nearby, Romeo of Villeneuve, count of Provence.

"Emperor Constantine turned
the Roman Eagle's course east by
transferring the seat of its power to
Byzantium, which reversed the westward
course it had followed under Aeneas.   5
More than two hundred years passed,
with its seat there at the edge of Europe,
passing from hand to hand, until I came
into power and moved it back west to Ravenna.

"I was 'Caesar' then and I am Justinian.   10
Inspired by the Primal Love I feel, I worked
to organize and purge what was unnecessary from
the laws of Rome. Earlier, I had believed that
Christ's nature was Divine and I was satisfied.
But the blessed Agapetus, who was Pope at   15
the time, converted me through his words and
showed me the true nature of Christ—human
as well as Divine. I heard his words and believed
him and now can clearly see the truth of his
teachings, which so obviously contradict   20
and disprove my earlier beliefs.

"As soon as I joined and began to follow the
Church, God's grace inspired me to my noble
task and I devoted myself to it. I left the duties of
war to my General Belisarius. Since Heaven's   25
right hand favored him, I considered it a sign
that I should turn my attention to other things.

"So that's the short answer to your first question.
But it leads to other things, and so maybe I
should try to explain a little better so that you   30
can see for yourself how unjustified both the
Guelfs and Ghibellines are when they fight,
whether against the Imperial symbol or claiming it for
their own. And so that you can see what virtues made
Rome worth revering, let's begin way back when the   35
Trojan Pallas died so that he might gain a kingdom.

CANTO VI, 28–30: JUSTINIAN'S ORATION:

*"So that's the short answer to your first question.
But it leads to other things, and so maybe I
should try to explain a little better."*

"You already know that it was more than three
hundred years after its founding in Alba before
the three Curiatii were defeated by the three
Horatii. And I'm sure you're well aware that   40
Rome expanded under seven emperors, from
the rape of the Sabines at the time of Romulus, all
the way up to the suicide of Lucrece. How, under
the leadership of famous Romans, it defeated
Brennus and restrained Pyrrhus, among others.   45

"And how Torquatus, Quintius (named
for his wild hair), the Decii, and the Fabii,
all won their fame, which I happily honor. And
when the Arabs crossed the rocky Alps with
Hannibal following the course of the Po River,   50
how they were defeated. It was under Rome that
both Scipio and Pompey triumphed, even though
they were young. (It must have seemed pretty
harsh to those that lived near where you were born.)

"Then, about the time of the birth of Christ, when Heaven   55
wanted to bring peace to the world, Caesar was elected
as Emperor of Rome. His victories under the Eagle
standard stretched across Gaul, from the Var River in the
east to the Rhine on the north and all the lands between
the Isère, Saône, and Seine rivers that drain to the Rhône.   60

"And you know, Caesar crossed the Rubicon,
attacking Pompey with such success that
stories and written accounts can't begin to
describe it. He led his troops into Spain and
on toward Durazzo, defeating Pompey so badly   65
at Pharsalia that he fled all the way to Egypt.

"Chasing Pompey, he returned to his birthplace,
Antandros and Simois, then detoured to Troy
—where Hector lies buried—and on to Egypt,
to Ptolemy's regret. He attacked Juba like   70
lightning, and then Caesar returned to
Spain to finish off Pompey and his followers.

"Augustus was next to raise Rome's Eagle banner,
   and because of him Brutus and Cassius now suffer
   in Hell and Modena and Perugia wallowed in grief.   75
   Because of him Cleopatra is still crying—as she
   fled from him she chose the fast and frightful
   death of the viper. And under Augustus the Eagle of
   Rome stretched to the very shores of the Red Sea,
   bringing a peace across the whole of the Roman Empire   80
   so the gates of the temple of Janus could be finally shut.

"But even all the things that were done under the Eagle
   of Augustus, the stuff I've been talking about so far—
   and even the stuff I haven't even mentioned yet—all that
   stuff pales in comparison to what was done under the   85
   reign of the third Caesar, as anyone with a clear mind
   and a pure heart can see. The true Justice of God
   that inspires me, granted to Tiberius the glory of
   avenging His own anger at Adam through the
   crucifixion of Christ, reconciling man with God.   90

"But there's more, check this out:
   It was under Titus that Rome sped toward
   avenging the vengeance of that very sin.
   And when the teeth of the Lombards snapped at the
   Holy Church, it was Charlemagne who rode under   95
   the Eagle banner to her aid through his victories.

"Now you yourself can be the judge of all
   those that I've mentioned, and decide how they
   have offended and the results of their crimes,
   which cause you troubles even to this day.   100

"The Guelfs oppose the Eagle under the yellow
   lilies of the house of France; the Ghibellines have
   adopted the Eagle as their own—it's hard to
   decide which is worse. The Ghibellines should
   choose another emblem, because separating   105
   the Eagle from its real meaning shows that they
   don't respect it. And this new guy, Charles II,
   shouldn't attack them either, or he'll feel the claws of

the Eagle himself. Sons have frequently suffered for
their fathers' mistakes, and he better not think that   110
God is gonna switch sides from the Eagle to the lilies.

"This little planet Mercury here—the Second Heaven—
is filled with the souls of those who acted for the
honor and fame that their deeds would bring them.
But when one's good deeds are bent by the desires   115
for Earthly gains, then the rays of true love are deflected
and bent as well to strike with a weaker beam.

"But part of our pleasure comes in measuring
one's rewards with their merits, and yet we see
that our rewards are no better or worse. And that's   120
how Living Justice makes all our affections so
sweet, now that they can never be twisted again
by lusts or unfulfilled desires. Just as various
voices join to form the music of a choir,
our different positions here in Heaven make   125
the Spheres of Paradise spin in harmony.

"And in this same pearl the soul of Romeo glows, a guy
whose good works were greeted by skepticism in his own
time. And the Provençals who conspired against him have
little to celebrate now, because those who have personal   130
problems with the good work of others are on the wrong
road to begin with. After all, all four of Raymond Berenger's
daughters ended up becoming queen anyway, and that all
came about because of poor, wandering Romeo. Even so,
Berenger was persuaded by another to call him to accounts   135
—the same guy would take ten from one guy and gave
Raymond five and seven. And in the end, old Romeo chucked
it all and left rather than stick around and be doubted.

"And if people knew what a good guy he was
as he sat begging, coin by coin, for his living   140
—even though they praise him now—they would
praise him a lot more if they knew the whole story."

CANTO VII

ARGUMENT

In the Second Heaven of Mercury, Justinian sings a Latin hymn as he finishes explaining everything to Dante, and then disappears into space. Dante is confused and Beatrice anticipates his questions: If Christ's Crucifixion is a "just revenge" for Adam's original sin, then why do the Jews deserve to be punished for it (through the destruction of Jerusalem)? Why is "just revenge" avenged? Beatrice explains that Adam's pride was man's sin, and Christ died on the Cross as vengeance for it. This was just as far as Jesus' human nature was concerned, but as far as God and Divine Nature is concerned, the punishment wasn't fair and therefore the Jews were punished. "Then why did God choose this way to redeem mankind?" Dante wonders. Beatrice answers that it was the most worthy way, and explains how God achieved man's redemption in two ways: through His Mercy—taking on human form—and through His Justice—death on the Cross. She explains that the compounds and elements—secondary things—aren't eternal because God didn't directly create them, and the canto closes with her alluding to the resurrection of the body after the Last Judgment.

*"H osanna, holy God of hosts,
illuminating from above
all the souls of Heaven!"*

Justinian sang these words and twirled
around to the beat until his glowing soul   5
and its two separate lights fused into one.
All the other souls joined him in the dance,
and then all of a sudden the whole lot of them
shot off and disappeared straight up into space.

But I was still confused, and even though a voice   10
in my head was saying, "Talk to her! Ask her!
She always knows the answers to everything!"
I was so in awe of her that even just hearing
the syllables *"BE"* or *"ICE"* was enough to make
me blush and bow my head like a shy teenager.   15

But, as always, she knew what I was going
through in my head and the smile she gave me
would have cheered you up on your deathbed.

"I can see you're struggling with the
question of why just vengeance needs to   20
be avenged itself," she said. "But don't fret—
calm down and let me explain. And listen
closely to my explanations, because it's
a whole set of guidelines for essential truth.

"Adam was selfish and did whatever he   25
wanted. Since he couldn't obey the rules God
set down, Adam, the first man, not only
condemned himself but all his offspring
as well. As a result, the entire human race
suffered down on Earth for centuries, until   30
Jesus was sent to spread God's word across
the world. Motivated only by His own love for man,
Jesus reclaimed human nature—which had
been lost by Adam's fall—for everyone. You
see," she continued, "human nature was   35
a gift from God. Adam had Free Will, which was

CANTO VII, 19–21: BEATRICE'S EXPLANATIONS:
"I can see you're struggling with the question of why just vengeance needs to be avenged itself," she said.

pure and without sin. But it was this Free Will
that caused him to disobey God, and why
he was kicked out of the Garden of Eden.

"Jesus united the Divine and human natures.   40
Think about that. Human nature was again
united to God, but it was human nature that had
distanced itself from God through Adam's act,
banished from Paradise by its Free Will. So, as Jesus
was human, the act of Crucifixion was a just penalty   45
for the sins of human nature. But, as Christ was Divine,
it was unforgivable. This public event produced entirely
different results, with both God and the Jews pleased—
but of course for completely opposite reasons. So the
concept of 'just' vengeance on the Jews—avenged by   50
Titus destroying Jerusalem—should be understandable.

"Now I see your brain is all tangled with
questions bunched up in there and you're
waiting for me to loosen the knot. You're
thinking, 'I completely understand what you said,   55
but I still don't get why God didn't choose some
other way to make amends for Adam's fall and
our redemption.' Listen closely: the reason for
God's choice in this manner of redemption is only
visible to those who have His Love in their   60
heart. But, since a lot of people struggle with
this and almost no one gets it, I'll explain
to you why God's choice is the best one.

"Divine Goodness burns brightly, but humbly,
and we're all born from God's spark and carry   65
a bit of His brightness with us wherever we go.
Everything that comes directly from God—that is
to say, angels and men—have an eternal tattoo
that, once inked, can never be removed. And,
because angels and men come directly from   70
Him, they're not subject to the laws and rules of
animals and plants and other secondary things.
Put it this way: What is most like God is the
most pleasing to God; the Sacred Flame
burns hottest in what is most similar to it.   75

"These are all the gifts humans were given.
And if they somehow fail in any one of these,
they fall from their blessed and noble position.
Sin is actually the only thing that takes away
man's Free Will and his likeness to God, as well
as dimming whatever brightness he may have had.

80

"And the only way to get any of that glow back
is to fill up the dark void left by sin and illicit acts
with some kind of fair amends and atonement.
See, when human nature sinned through Adam,
way back in the beginning, it was expelled from
these great honors and kicked out of the Garden.

85

"And if you think about it for a second," she
continued, "there was no way man could recover
what Adam had lost, except through either of
these two options: either God, just because He's
so forgiving, had to pardon the sin, or man himself
had to figure out a way to pay for his own mistake.

90

"Now look into the Heavens and concentrate
on God's image while I explain this part.
It gets tricky, so pay attention as best you can.

95

"Given their built-in limitations," she lectured,
"there's no way that humans could make amends—
man's simply not humble enough, and no apology
would ever be as deep as the heights that Adam
had been trying to reach through his sin.
So man could never make amends to God.

100

"So that left it up to God, then, through
either Justice or Mercy (or both) to bring
man back around. And because any act
becomes more important the more it reflects
the gracious and loving heart of the doer, when
God—whose fingerprints can be seen on all
the things of the world—decided to redeem
man, He was happy and ready to do so.

105

110

"From the time of creation to the Final
Judgment there has never been—and

never will be—an act so magnificent
and glorious as what He did. God gave
Jesus so humans could raise themselves up   115
and go to Paradise, which was way more
valuable than just letting Him forgive them.
If God's only Son didn't humble Himself and
take on human flesh and blood, any other attempt
at redemption wouldn't have been enough.   120

"And just to take care of all your questions,
I'll back up and explain what I meant when I
mentioned the secondary things," she continued.
"You're probably saying to yourself, 'It's obvious
that fire and water and Earth and stuff don't   125
seem to last too long before they start to fall
apart. But aren't all of these things also God's
creations? I thought what you said before
meant that they'd all be safe against decay.'

"Well here's your answer: People and angels—   130
and even this place you are now—were all
created just as they appear, unchanging and
complete. But the elements you're talking about,
and everything that comes from them as well,
are created by secondary forces. Those kinds of   135
things are all created by Heavenly influences, not
God, as are all the decisions made in the stars
and constellations that circle them. The souls of
all the animals and plants come from an inert
combination of elements, by the way the stars   140
move and the powers that emanate from
them. But when God gives a human being
life, he fills it up with the kind of love that
thirsts after Him, what we call First Love.

"So," she said, sighing, "following this logic,   145
you should be able to grasp the concept of
resurrection. All you need to remember is how
bodies were created as in the case of Adam and Eve."

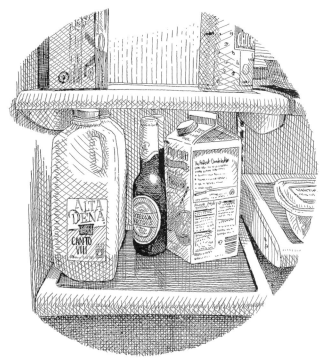

CANTO VIII

ARGUMENT

Dante and Beatrice float from Mercury up to the Sphere of Venus so fast that the only way he knows they're moving is when he sees Beatrice becoming more beautiful. Now in the Third Heaven, they are surrounded by the souls of those with such a disposition toward love that they yielded to it too much in life. They sing in Paradise now that they are purified in the afterlife. The soul of Charles Martel, a friend of Dante's, now comes forward. He explains to Dante how the Heavens influence men, and why human nature isn't passed along through families. Finally, he explains problems that occur when one's natural disposition is unrealized in life.

Back in pagan times the world believed
that it was the fair goddess Venus, risen
from the sea near Cyprus and spinning
in her orbit, who sends down the rays of
irresistible love to the world. That old   5
misconception led people to worship
her through sacrifices and prayer. And
not just her, but they worshiped her son,
Cupid, and her mother, Dione, as well.
And they named that planet—which flirts with   10
the sun, sometimes rising before it and other
times setting after it—after Venus as well.

I had no feeling of us rising up to it, but I was
sure that we had reached the Sphere of Venus
when I noticed that Beatrice had become even   15
more beautiful than before. And just like you
can see individual sparks when you look at a fire,
or how sometimes you can hear one voice standing
out from a bunch of them in a choir, I could make
out other lights spinning around us in the glow,   20
all at different speeds, probably having
their own reasons for being there.

Any gust of wind or bolt of lightning that has ever
shot down from the clouds would seem slow
in comparison to how fast those Heavenly lights   25
came at us, stopping the course that they had
begun up in the Primum Mobile among the Seraphim
angels to spin around us. A shout of *"Hosanna!"*
sounded from the ones in front so beautifully
that to this day I'm still dying to hear it again.   30

Then one of them came closer to us and said,
"We are all here at your service, only hoping to
make you happy. We spin together here as one,
united by our love and desire for God as we revolve
with the Principalities of the Angelic Intelligence,   35
about whom you once wrote, 'You who by your
thought move the Third Heaven,' in your book *Convivo*.

And we're so full of love that in making you happy,
a short pause will not seem less sweet."

My eyes, after I had first looked to my   40
girl to see if it was cool and after hers
had shown me that it was all OK, turned
back to the guy shining there before me
and I asked him as nicely as I could,
"Please, tell me—who are you?"   45

As I watched it seemed like the soul flared up and
grew even brighter than before as I spoke to him,
like I was piling happiness on top of his happiness.

And as he flared up like that he said, "I didn't
last too long on Earth, but if I had lived longer,   50
a lot of bad stuff that's going on now would
have been avoided. The glow of my happiness
now shines in your eyes so that you can't see me
clearly, it wraps around me like a cocoon. You
loved me a lot when we met and had good reason;   55
if I had hung around longer I would have shown
more love to you than there are lights in Vegas.

"All the land west of the Rhône River below
where it joins the Sorgue would've been
under my rule if I had lived, as the southern   60
horn of Italy (called Ausonia back then) would
have been too—south of the Tronto and the
Garigliano rivermouths, bordered by the towns
of Catona, Bari, and Gaeta. The crown of Hungary,
where the Danube flows after leaving Germany,   65
had already been granted to me. And on that
stretch of coast most threatened by the Sirocco
winds, from Cape Passaro up to Cape Faro—
always overcast because of sulphur, not by the
rumblings of the volcano Typhoeus—fair Sicily   70
would still be awaiting its rulers, descended from
me and from Charles of Anjou and Rudolph of
Hapsburg, if bad governing (which always caused
its subjects to suffer) had not provoked the uprisings
in Palermo with all the shouts of 'Die! Die!'   75

CANTO VIII, 115–117: CHARLES MARTEL:

"Then let me ask you this," he said. "Would a person
on Earth be worse off if they weren't a part of a society?"
"Oh, for sure," I said, "you don't have to explain that."

"And if my brother could see what's coming,
he'd bail on Catalonia and all its needy
poverty before anything happens to him.
The boat of his responsibilities is already
so loaded that somebody better stop him   80
from taking on any more baggage. His
greediness is descended from a generous
father, and what he needs is the services of
soldiers not bent on filling their own pockets."

"My prince," I said to him now that I recognized   85
him, "I'm sure that with our vision—at the beginning
and ending of all good—you can tell how happy it
makes me to hear what you're saying. And knowing
you know makes me even happier. Plus, knowing
you're blessed up here and that you sensed it yourself   90
when you looked at God, well, that makes me happy too.
But now help me out here. You've got me wondering:
how it is that good families can have such lousy kids?"

"If you remember just one thing from me," he said,
"I'll do my best to lay this all out in front of you,   95
since you seem to have turned your back on
it up to now. You see, the Good that makes
these Spheres spin around—that you're rising up
through—is happy spreading providence as a
force in the Heavens to influence man. In His   100
perfect mind He makes sure that not only the
natures of his creations, but their well-being is
also provided for, giving every person a chance
to fulfill their place in the order of the universe.
Everyone has all the things necessary to stay on   105
target in life, like a laser from a pointer. If it wasn't like
that, things around here would be all wild and chaotic,
ending in destruction instead of positive results.
And that's impossible, because that would mean that
there is a flaw in the Primal One who made everything.   110

"Do you get it now," he asked, "or do I have to
make it even more simple for you understand?"

"No, it's pretty obvious to me that nature can't
lack what's necessary for itself," I answered.

"Then let me ask you this," he said. "Would a person   115
on Earth be worse off if they weren't a part of a society?"

"Oh, for sure," I said, "you don't have to explain that."

"So then, how can there be a society if people aren't
all different from each other, with everyone having different
jobs and stuff? There can't be, if what Aristotle wrote is right."   120

Having laid out his argument step by step so
far, he now wrapped it all up: "Since everyone's
different—right?—then the sources of their differences
must be different too. So, some are born destined
to be lawyers, some to be generals, another guy to   125
be a priest, someone else to be an inventor or a
mechanic. The spinning Heavens exert their
influences on human nature, like a thumbprint
on soft wax, but those traits don't have to do
with families. You can see that clearly in the   130
differences between Esau and Jacob, for example,
or in the case of Romulus, who was so unlike his
loser father that they said he must be the son of
Mars instead. If Divine Providence didn't get involved,
everyone would end up being just like their dad.   135

"Now I've placed the thing right in front of you
so you can see it clearly. And from the pure joy
that this conversation has brought me, let me
present you with a corollary: When nature comes
upon unfavorable circumstances, dispositions—   140
like seeds sown in the wrong climate—can't fulfill
their possibilities. If society would follow Heaven's
way of doing things, it would recognize each
person's worth. But instead you go and push
one guy toward religion when he would have   145
been more fit for politics, and make kings out of
people who would have been better off in the clergy.
That sends the whole train off the tracks."

CANTO IX

ARGUMENT

In the previous canto, Charles Martel made some bleak predictions about the future of his family, and Dante begins this canto with a note to Charles's wife, Clemence. Still in the Third Sphere of Venus, the soul of Cunizza da Romano appears before them and denounces her brother's bloody rule of her native lands, the March of Treviso, near Venice. She predicts a dire future, and drifts away after mentioning that someone famous is beside her. This is the soul of Folquet, who was once the Bishop of Toulouse. Like Cunizza, he too led a lustful life, but later became enamored with the love of God. He speaks about the nature of the Sphere of Venus and introduces Rahab, the Whore of Jericho, symbol of salvation through faith, who was one of the first to ascend to Heaven after the Crucifixion. He goes on to denounce Florence as a city grown from Satan's seed, whose money, the florin, has become the obsession of clergymen. In the end, he predicts that the Vatican itself will one day be purged of these adulterers of faith.

Beautiful Clemence, when your dear husband,
Charles, spoke to me, he told me about future
schemes that would destroy his family, but he
also told me not to tell anyone else about it.
All I can say is this: the people who mess   5
with you will get what they deserve in the end.

As he finished speaking, the glowing soul of
Charles Martel turned to face the sun, drinking
in the rays of His light like an electrical current.

Beware, you poor human souls, deceived   10
and proud, who turn away from the true
Good of God, and focus instead on emptiness.

Then another of those brilliant lights
floated over toward me. I could tell by
its glow that it was friendly and eager to   15
chat. Beatrice looked over and I could
see encouragement in her eyes, and I knew
that what I wanted to ask was OK with her.

"Blessed soul," I said to the light, "I bet
you're probably able to read my mind   20
and guess my questions already, right?"
And whoever it was, that soul answered
me in a voice full of kindness, as
beautiful in speech as it had been in song.

"In the northeast of sinful Italy, between Venice   25
and the Alps, where the Brenta and Piave rivers
are formed, there is a hill," the voice began.
"Ezzelino was born there, and went on, as predicted,
to conquer and torch the countryside. Of course
now he lies in Hell's river of boiling blood.   30

"He and I were born from the same parents.
My name was Cunizza, and you see me shining
here in Venus after a long life of love and passion.
But I have no regrets—all that was washed away by

CANTO IX, 32–34: CUNIZZA AND FOLQUET:

"My name was Cunizza, and you see me shining
here in Venus after a long life of love and passion.
But I have no regrets."

the River Lethe. I am here thanks to God's love and   35
forgiveness, which is probably hard for you to understand.

"And this beautiful soul who's shining beside
me is well-known to everyone up here in this Sphere,
and even more famous down on Earth. His fame
will last five centuries and more. He's an example   40
of what shooting for the stars will get you: your name
will live on and have a second life after you pass away.

"But of course those losers who live in the
March of Treviso couldn't care less about
that, or change their ways despite being   45
defeated. Their stubbornness will have
rivers running red with their Paduan blood,
because they have no loyalty at all to the Emperor.

"And the arrogant Riccardo da Cammino—who
rules over Treviso where the Sile and Cagnano   50
rivers meet—the trap for him is already set.

"The Bishop of Feltre will come to regret turning in
those Ghibelline refugees," she said, "and no one
has ever been sent up the river to Malta prison for a
more heinous crime than that. You'd need a swimming   55
pool to hold all the blood spilled by those poor Ghibs,
and trying to sort it out would be exhausting. Anyways,
the Bishop was happy to sacrifice all that blood for
his party, the Guelfs. But before he knows it,
bloodletting will become the way of life in his land.   60

"There are mirrors up in Saturn's Sphere—'Thrones,'
you'd probably call them—that reflect God's judgments,
which is why my prophecies might seem harsh to you."

As she finished, Cunizza seemed to become lost
in her own thoughts or something, and she drifted   65
back over to the dancing wheel of glowing souls.

The gleaming spark she had praised
came toward me then, as sparkling and
bright as sunlight on steel. In Paradise,

happiness makes the souls glow brighter,
just as it makes us smile on Earth, and
casts a shadow on the souls in Hell below.

"God sees everything," I said to him politely.
"And since you see through Him, I'm
sure you can see my thoughts as well.
I've heard your beautiful voice already when
you sang with the others, and it's right up
there with the Angels of Divine Love,
the Seraphim. Why do you wait to answer
my questions, then? I certainly wouldn't wait
very long if I was as in you as you're in me."

"The Mediterranean Sea is the greatest
valley on Earth," he answered, "and the
Atlantic Ocean flows into it at Gibraltar.
It's so big that at its eastern shore
near Jerusalem, its westernmost
point, is beyond the horizon. The town
I was born in lies in the valley between
the Ebro River in Spain and the Magra
River that divides the Genoese and
the Tuscans in Italy. Directly south of
my hometown is Bougie, on the African
coast, which was once invaded by Caesar.

"I'm from Marseilles, and people who knew me
called me Folquet. I was influenced by this Sphere
in life, even as it accepts me in death. By seducing
Aeneas, Dido wronged both her husband, Sichaeus,
and Aeneas's wife, Creusa, but even her lust didn't
burn as bright as mine did. Nor did Phyllis's love
compare when it drove her to suicide when Demophoön
didn't show for their wedding. My love was more
than even Hercules' when he ran off with Iole.

"But here we do not regret, we smile," he said.
"Not at the sin itself, of course, but at the
power of God's love, and at the contemplation

70

75

80

85

90

95

100

105

and art of his creation. From up here, we can see
how the Spheres work so effectively, see how the
Heavens above form and reflect the world below.

"But if I'm going to answer all the questions
you have about this place to your satisfaction,   110
I'd better start addressing them.

"You want to know who it is that flickers
here beside me like a sparkler in July.
This is Rahab, once called the Whore
of Jericho, who finally has peace here.   115
Since she joined this Sphere she has
held its highest rank. She was the first
soul to arrive here in Venus, on the far
reaches of the Earth's shadow, with all the
souls brought upward after the Crucifixion.   120
And it's fitting that she resides in this
Sphere as symbolic of Christ's victory
because it was Rahab who made it possible
for Joshua to take Jericho, his first win in
the Holy Land—though that doesn't seem   125
to matter much to the Pope nowadays.

"Your city of Florence—which grew from the
seed of Lucifer, the first to turn his back on
God and whose bitter envy has wreaked havoc
on the world—is where they mint the florins.   130
Those damned, lily-stamped coins turn priests
into greedy wolves who neglect their flock and
leave them to wander astray. For love of money
the Bible is ignored and the disciples are forgotten
while the clergymen are obsessed with the money   135
to be made from their dog-eared copies of Canon Law.

"The Cardinals and the Pope think of nothing else!
They forget the lessons of humility shown by Gabriel
at his appearance to Mary in Nazareth. But don't worry.
Soon the Vatican, site of St. Peter's martyrdom   140
and burial ground of saints, will be rid of these
adulterers, free from this corruption and greed!"

CANTO X

ARGUMENT

Dante and Beatrice rise imperceptibly to the Fourth Heaven, the Sphere of the Sun, where those wise on Earth now appear. Beatrice explains how even the seeming imperfections in the order of the universe reflect God's hand. A ring of twelve lights appears and spins about them, and when the lights stop, one voice introduces himself as St. Thomas Aquinas. He goes around the circle and introduces the other spirits.

As He looked upon His Son with the love that
gushes from all three of Them, the Force—
uncreatable and inexplicable—organized everything
that spins around in space; and even inside your
head too, so if you stop to think about it, you   5
can't help but get a sense of Him from it all.

Well then, Reader, lift your eyes to Aries above,
where I'm looking, and watch how the Heavens spin.
See how one orbit crosses another, and you'll begin
to see how well it was all made. You'll see the art of the   10
Master, which loves it so much that He never takes
His eyes off it (or off Himself). Check out how the
paths of the planets through the Zodiac are all a bit
off kilter, like branches coming out of a tree trunk, in
order to meet the demands that the world makes on them.   15
If the Earth's orbit wasn't a little tweaked, or if
it was tilted too much, a lot of the Heavenly power
of the Sun would be wasted, and almost all the power
on Earth would be dead. And if the path of the Zodiac
wobbled from its course, then the balance of the   20
Earth would be disrupted in both hemispheres.

Now before you get up from your chair, Reader,
stop and ponder what you've just had a taste
of; it will give you a lot of pleasure before you
get bored. I've prepared the plate for you,   25
now dig in. The stuff I'm trying to write
about here demands my full attention.

The Sun, nature's most important administrator—
the one who stamps the Earth with Heaven's
force and whose light provides the measurement   30
of time—was directly overhead in Aries, spinning
across the spirals of spring, when he dawns
earlier every day. And I was with him, but had
no more sensation of rising than you have of
the time between the moment an idea forms   35
in your head and its arrival in your brain. And
guiding me along from good to better was
Beatrice, flying us along so quickly that we
arrived even at the moment we had begun.

The lights I saw as we entered the Sun were   40
so bright that I can't remember any color at all,
only a kind of brilliance. All my vocabulary, writing
skills, and years of experience can't help me describe
it so that you can picture it. You'll just have to
take my word for it—and hope that you'll get to   45
see it for yourself one day. Actually, it shouldn't
be a surprise if our minds can't picture it, because
no eyes can look at light brighter than the Sun's.

That is what the Fourth Sphere was like. It's where the
spirits of the wise appeared, satisfied at last, able to   50
comprehend the mysteries of how He has a Son,
and how each of them breathes for the Spirit.

"Give thanks to the Sun of the Angels," Beatrice said,
"Thanks that He has raised you here by His grace."

No one's heart was so ready to   55
totally devote itself to thankfulness
than mine was at that moment. I was so
overeager that, when I heard her words,
I immediately focused so much love on
Him that I completely forgot about Beatrice.   60

But she didn't care. She actually smiled when
she saw it, and the beauty of her eyes split
my love between the two loves I felt at once.

Around us I saw lights moving brilliantly.
We were in the middle and they surrounded   65
us, with voices even more amazing than their
light. It was like the hazy glow that surrounds
Latona's daughter Diana, the Moon,
when the fog at night catches her light.

In the courts of Paradise—where I've been and come   70
back from—there are so many indescribable and precious
jewels so unique that they can't be taken out of Heaven's
care. One such jewel was the song those spirits sang.
To hear it for yourself you'll have to fly to Paradise,
or else wait to hear it from the mouths of the dumb.   75

CANTO X, 99–102: IN THE SPHERE OF THE SUN:
"I am Thomas of Aquino.
If you want to know the others, I'll introduce
them, so let your eyes follow as my words
lead you around this sacred circle."

And as they sang, the burning spirits circled
us three times, horizontally, like stars
above the North Pole, and it seemed to
me that, even as they ended their song,
slowly, they were always on the verge   80
of busting out again at any moment.

Then I heard a voice rise from one of the souls.
"Because the light of grace shines inside
you with that love that, once it's been
kindled, can only expand; and because   85
it has led you up the stairs that, once you've
climbed them you have to climb them again,
we're not able to resist the pull of your
thirst for knowledge any more than
water can resist going downhill.   90

"I can tell you're dying to know what
flowers we are that bloom here in this
garden that surrounds you and your lovely
guide on your ascent through Paradise,"
he said. "I was a sheep in the holy flock of   95
the Dominican Order—where one may grow
fatter if you don't stray from the path.
On my right here is both my teacher and my brother,
Albert from Cologne. I am Thomas of Aquino.
If you want to know the others, I'll introduce   100
them, so let your eyes follow as my words
lead you around this sacred circle.

"The next gleam over comes from the smile of
Gratian, whose writings joined religious and secular
laws so well that his work is admired, even in Heaven.   105

"The next one over in our group is Peter,
who likened his own book, *Sentences*, to
the offerings of a poor widow to the church.

"The fifth light over is the brightest among us,
Solomon, whose *Song of Songs* expresses   110
such love that everyone down there wants news
of him. In that soul there is a mind so profoundly

wise that, if the truth be known, no one ever
arrived up here with so much vision as him.

"The light of the next bulb burns with   115
the soul of one who understands the
nature of the Angelic Orders. Meet Dionysius.

"And the next flicker beside him sparks with
the soul of Paulus Orosius, whose writings
championed Christianity, encouraged by Augustine.   120

"Now, if you've kept up with me, you should
be looking at the eighth lamp over there,
dying to know who he is. That sparkle
contains Boethius, whose writings on
philosophy expose the deceits of the   125
world if you read them well. His body
lies buried below in Cieldauro in Pavia,
and he joins us here after his martyrdom
and exile. Say hello, Boethius.

"The next three flames around," he continued, "are those   130
of Isidore of Seville, Bede, and Richard of St. Victor,
whose meditations made him more than a man.

"And the last light before you get to me again
is that of a serious spirit who knew sorrow and
wished for a sooner death than he had.   135
He is Sigier, who taught in Paris on the
Rue de Fouarre, where he defended
certain truths, as his logic led him to do."

Then, like the bells of a church at dawn
as they call the faithful to get up and to   140
worship, inspiring love of Him through
the pleasing notes of their ringing—each
note seeming to fill you with more love—
I watched that glorious wheel of sparkling
souls spin slowly and burst again into   145
songs so lovely and harmonious that
they can never be re-created outside
of that place where happiness is eternal.

CANTO XI

ARGUMENT

Safely up in the Sphere of the Sun, Dante criticizes humans for their useless pursuits on Earth below. In the previous canto, Thomas Aquinas said "one may grow fatter if you don't stray" in the Dominican Order, and toward the end of this one, he explains the corruption that allows it. In between, he tells the love story of St. Francis and Lady Poverty and how the Pope sanctioned the Franciscan Order in 1223.

(Humankind is so frickin' hopeless, full
of worthless, left-brained logic that ends
up keeping people down when they try to rise
to higher goals. Some men are eager to
become lawyers or doctors, others aim for the   5
priesthood, and others claw their way up the
political shitpile for power. Some men turn to
violent crime while others are white-collar
criminals. Some people are pimps, some are
porn stars, and many are just plain lazy. And   10
there I was, side by side with Beatrice up in
Paradise, welcomed by everyone up there.)

When each of the souls had gone back
to their places in the circle, they all stopped,
flickering like candles in a birthday cake.   15
Then the soul of St. Thomas Aquinas
hovered before me again, and spoke to me
like a smile, growing brighter all the time.

"Just as God's rays shine through me,
I'm able to look into you and see exactly   20
what you're thinking and where you're
doubting. I have confused you, and you
want me to break it down and explain
what I meant earlier in very simple terms.

"I said 'one may grow fatter if you don't stray' and   25
'no one ever arrived up here with so much vision,'
and now I see that we need to make a distinction.

"Providence governs the world with
wisdom so deep and profound that
no one could ever try to get to the   30
bottom of it. The Church is the Bride
of Christ, wedded to Him through His
blood on the Cross as their wedding vows.
And Providence sent two great princes,
Francis and Dominic, to help carry the   35
Church, one for each shoulder, like guides.

"Francis is famous for the intensity of his love,
like the angels of the Seraphic Order, while
Dominic is known for his wisdom, like the Cherubs.
I'm only going to speak about Francis right now,   40
but it doesn't really matter, because praising one
is the same as both, as they had equal goals.

"Between the Tupino and Chiascio rivers, and
below Mt. Subasio, where Ubaldo lived as a
recluse, there is a fertile hill. The town of Assisi   45
lies in the shadow of the mountains there, while
across the valley the town of Perugia's Porta Sole
faces it, and over the ridge the towns of Gualdo
and Nocera are exposed to the brunt of the weather.
Francis was born on that steep slope, rising into the   50
world as bright as the Sun does over the Ganges River.
But, given the son who was raised there, it would be
more appropriate to call the town Orient than Assisi,
since the Sun always rises in the east and is so bright.

"It wasn't long before the power of   55
his influence was evident to the world
around him. He was still young when,
in 1207, in front of the Bishop of Assisi and
his father, Francis gave up his inheritance
and embraced a vow to Lady Poverty—   60
that woman who everyone avoids like death.
It was a marriage of love that only grew
as the years went by. Since the loss of
her first husband on the Cross, Poverty
had been neglected and ridiculed and   65
despised for nearly eleven hundred years.

"Men didn't find her appealing even when
she was with Lucan, the fisherman so poor
that he had nothing to fear from Caesar's
plundering troops. And her courage to stay   70
at Jesus' side on the Cross, while Mary stayed
below, didn't win her many converts either.

"But not to dwell on it too depressingly, the
    point is that Francis and Poverty are the
    lovers in the story I'm telling. They were
    so deeply connected and devoted that their
    faces shone with a glow, and their hearts
    were overwhelmed with sacred thoughts.

"A wealthy merchant named Bernard became
    the first to follow Francis, kicking off his shoes
    and selling everything as he went. And even
    though he went running, it seemed slow to him.
    He was followed by Giles and Sylvester, who
    chucked their possessions for spiritual wealth.

"Finally, Francis and his Bride and all his followers
    set out for Rome to seek approval of their Order
    wearing nothing but sackcloth with rope for belts.
    He wasn't intimidated or uptight about the fact
    that his father, Bernardone, was a rich shopkeeper,
    and he wasn't ashamed of his shabby clothes at all.
    He strode right in there as if he was royalty
    and gave the hard sell to Pope Innocent III, who
    verbally sanctioned the Order of St. Francis.

"The number of people who followed Francis into
    poverty kept growing and growing, until he—
    whose wondrous and exemplary life should've
    been sung by Heaven's highest angels—was
    granted a written sanction by Pope Honorius III
    in 1223, all through God's great graces.

"In 1224, he went to Egypt with the Fifth Crusade
    and preached the truth of Christ to the Sultan,
    who received him kindly, but didn't really listen.
    He had trouble finding any converts there, and
    since he didn't want to waste his whole trip, he
    went back to see what he could do in Italy. And
    while he was fasting on Mt. Alvernia, between the
    rivers Arno and Tiber, he received the marks of
    Christ's wounds, which he carried to his death.

75

80

85

90

95

100

105

CANTO XI, 133–136: THOMAS OF AQUINO:

"So, if my long speech hasn't been too arcane,
and if you've been listening carefully the whole time,
and remember what I said back in the beginning,
you realize your questions have been answered."

"When God in Heaven finally decided
      that it was time to call him home and   110
      up to the rewards that he so deserved,
Francis commended the care of Lady Poverty
      to his followers and rightful heirs. He was
      then taken to the remote church of Porziuncola,
where he asked to be stripped bare and   115
      chose to die naked on bare earth,
      where the soul is closer to Heaven.

"Now just think just for a second what kind
      of man it would take to partner with Francis
      and guide St. Peter's boat, keeping it on   120
the true course" he said. "That sailor is our
      Patriarch, Dominic. Anyone who follows
      him will soon see how rich his cargo is.
But his crew is getting greedier now,
      wandering far in search of food, distracted   125
      in foreign lands. And the farther they
travel off into the world, the more distant,
      the less healthy they seem when they
      return to the fold. There are still a few
who are a bit scared and stay close to their   130
      keeper, but so few, really, that it wouldn't
      take much to feed and clothe them.

"So, if my long speech hasn't been too arcane,
      and if you've been listening carefully the whole time,
      and remember what I said back in the beginning,   135
you realize your questions have been answered.
      The tree of the Dominican Order has been spiked,
      and you now realize what I meant when I said,
'one may grow fatter if you don't stray.'"

CANTO XII

ARGUMENT

Dante and Beatrice are still in the Fourth Heaven of the Sun when a second ring of twelve sparkling flames now appears surrounding the first one. A voice from one of them gives a long speech in praise of St. Dominic. This is Bonaventure of Bagnorea, a Franciscan. He tells about the life of Dominic, then rants about how the Franciscan Order is straying from the correct path. Finally, he introduces himself, then goes around the circle introducing the other spirits burning with him, most of whom were followers of St. Francis.

Just as the holy flame finished speaking, the
whole wheel of lights began to revolve. But even
before it had made a complete turn, another ring
of lights appeared surrounding the first one,
turning as well, matching its speed and its   5
song. The music was so much more beautiful
than the music of our own Earthly Muses and
Sirens that they seem pale in comparison—almost
like reflected light when compared to its source.

It was like when Juno commands her   10
maid Iris, the rainbow, to appear in the
clouds and two appear at once. The first
is slightly dimmer, a shadow of the second.
Think for a second of Echo, consumed
by her love for Narcissus or like mist and fog   15
overwhelmed by the Sun. (And think of the rainbow
reminding man of God's promise to Noah
that He will never flood the world again.)
Those two rings of eternal light circled
around us like two rainbows—   20
the outer circle echoing the first.

The celestial dance and celebration, that
dazzle of lights inside of lights, fire in fire,
happiness in benevolence, instantly
stopped and fell silent, as if with one mind.   25
It reminded me of how our two eyes work
together but are controlled by only one brain.
Then I heard a voice coming from one of
the new lights, and I felt pulled toward it like a
compass needle is pulled toward the North Star.   30

"Out of love and fairness I feel compelled to
speak about the other leader," it began, "who
has given so much praise to others up 'til now.
As we're all here, it is only right that we introduce
each other, having fought side by side on Earth.   35
Let us now share in glory and shine together.

CANTO XII, 19–21: AMONG THE WISE:
> *Those two rings of eternal light circled*
> *around us like two rainbows—*
> *the outer circle echoing the first.*

"Once humanity, Christ's army, had been redeemed
at the heavy price of His sacrifice, it was slow and
unsure of itself, barely gathered behind the Cross.
God, the Eternal Commander, helped His troops,   40
threatened by the danger of eternal sin, by giving His own
Son out of His own goodness (not because they deserved it).
And, as you already know, He sent reinforcements to
the Church, giving her two leaders who could bring hope
to His struggling people—two who would inspire by their   45
example and their teaching: St. Francis and St. Dominic.

"In the far West," he continued, "where the
soft winds come from that blow the breath
of spring to reawaken Europe, near the coast
of Spain, pounded by Atlantic swells and   50
beyond which the Sun sets from the eyes
of all men after its longest day, you'll find the
town of Calaroga in the kingdom of Castile,
whose coat of arms shows two castles and two
lions, one above and the other below. It was within   55
those walls that St. Dominic was born, champion of the
Christian faith, loving of his own, tough on his foes.

"Soon after his very conception his mind
was so full of life that even while inside
his mother's womb he filled her with   60
prophetic powers. At his baptism, where he
wedded faith and brought mutual salvation
to the union, the rites of their joining
were sealed. In a dream, his godmother
foresaw the amazing fruit that would come   65
from him and his heirs. And so that his
name might correspond to his deeds,
a spirit from Heaven was sent down so
that he would be known by the possessive
form of the One by whom he was possessed   70
completely. He was named Dominic. I think
of him as a gardener chosen by Christ
to work in His garden, the Church.

"From the beginning," he went on, "he seemed
to be the perfect choice for a servant of Christ: 75
Dominic's first love followed Jesus' first counsel.
As an infant, his nanny would find him lying still
and alert, with an expression on his face that
seemed to say, 'This is why I'm here.'

"Even his father, Felice, and his mother, Giovanna   80
(from the Hebrew for 'full of grace'), are also aptly
named, if it's true that, as they say, the name makes
the man. Unlike those who study Enrico da Susa's writing
on the Pope's Decretals rather than the Scriptures, or those
who follow the teachings of Taddeo d'Alderotto, Dominic   85
dedicated himself to learning out of a love of knowledge,
not for Earthly gain. He quickly became such a great
teacher that he became Pope, nurturing the Church and
caring for its vines, which had been neglected so long
by others. And as the head of that Institution—which was   90
once much kinder to the poor than now, under its current
leader Boniface VIII, who ignores them—he never asked
for his rightly dispensation to be deducted from payments
to the poor, not for the first benefice that opened up, not even
for the tithes 'that belong to God's poor.' All he asked for was   95
the right to preach to the wayward, sowing the seeds that grew
into the twenty-four blossoms of light that now surround you.

"And so he went at it," the voice continued,
"his eagerness combining with his knowledge,
rushing like a flood at the places where the   100
thorny bushes of his detractors grew the
thickest. And from this torment the many
streams that now water the Catholic garden
have flowed, so that its plants now
grow greener, their roots deeper.   105

"And if Dominic's life has been one wheel
of the chariot of the Holy Church that took
to the battlefield against her enemies, then
you'll easily recognize the excellence of the
other wheel, St. Francis, whom Thomas was   110

going on about just before we got here. But
even now, the path that wheel forged is being
abandoned, like a golf ball lost in the bushes.
His family, the Franciscans, who had been following
in his footsteps, has turned back, retreating step by   115
step, the first foot now following instead of leading.

"And you'll soon see, when it comes time
for the harvest, that the crop has been poor
and there won't be any place in the storage
bins of paradise for the unhealthy stalks.   120

"Oh sure, if you were to go through
our Order like a book, page by page,
you'd still find one that remained true.
But those that follow under the leadership
of Acquasparta or Casale seem to be   125
playing fast and loose with the rules.

"I am the burning spirit of Bonaventure of
Bagnorea," he finally explained. "I myself
always put the spiritual things before the Earthly
ones. And with me here are Illuminato da Rieti   130
and Augustine of Assisi—they were two
of the first, poor followers of Francis.

"Next to them you'll see Hugh of St. Victor;
then there's Peter of Spain, whose twelve
books have been very influential down below.   135
Next is Peter the Reader, then there's Nathan the
Prophet, Anselm, and John Chrysostom the Metropolitan.
After him is Donatus, who taught the art of grammar.

"Old Rabanus is here with us," he said, gesturing,
"and next to me sparkles the Calabrian Abbot   140
Joachim with his prophecies on the Holy Spirit.

"The glowing praise and kindness of Thomas's
words were what urged me to come and add to
the praises of St. Dominic, and this inspired the
rest of this group to appear before you as well."   145

CANTO XIII

ARGUMENT

Dante begins this canto by attempting to give readers a visual of the brilliance that surrounds him. Then Thomas Aquinas returns to explain that, while Adam and Jesus were the wisest beings ever created because they came directly from God, King Solomon was without equal in wisdom because he asked for understanding and was prudent, not rash or overly intellectual. Aquinas finishes the canto by warning people not to make quick judgments and hasty decisions, citing a few historical examples of people who rushed to judgment or based their thinking on false premises. Finally, he warns people not to be quick to judge others, as that should be reserved for God.

Those of you who are following along and want
a visual, try to imagine this description and
keep it focused in your mind's eye as you read:

Picture the fifteen brightest stars in all the
Heavens, the ones that are so bright their   5
light can cut through the thickest clouds; add
to them the seven glittering stars of the
Big Dipper, which you can always see in the
sky of the Northern Hemisphere; and finally,
add the two brightest stars of the Little Dipper,   10
whose tip is the North Star—which acts as the
axis for the revolutions of the Primum Mobile.

Now picture all of those stars arranged into
two huge double constellations, like Ariadne's
crown—a glowing wreath of twenty-four stars.   15
Imagine them as two rings, one inside the
other, the wheels turning in opposite directions,
all spinning around in space with me in the
center. Imagine this and you may get some
slight shadow of an idea about the constellation   20
of lights that were circling me. A faint idea,
since the true vision is as far beyond our
human comprehension as a bullet train
passing a mule cart on a country road.

And those souls were singing. Not about   25
Bacchus or Apollo, but about the Holy Trinity,
and in praise of the dual nature of Jesus Christ.

When their song ended, those sacred,
gleaming souls stopped spinning and all
turned to look at us, beaming with happiness.   30
Their holy and perfect silence was broken
by the kind voice of Thomas Aquinas, who'd
just finished telling the story of St. Francis.

"Now that we've solved one of the questions that's
bugging you, and you've had time to digest it,   35
let's see what we can do about the other one.

"I know that in your mind you believe that Adam—
whose rib was used to form the lovely Eve
(whose sweet tooth led to man's ruin)—
and Jesus—who was nailed to the Cross as
penance for man's past and future sins,
managing to absolve us all from guilt—had
to have been the wisest creatures that God
ever created. And you're right. He gave them as
much wisdom as human nature could possibly
contain. And so of course you were surprised
when I spoke about Solomon, the fifth light here,
and how his wisdom was the greatest. Well,
then: open your eyes wide to what I'm about to
show you, and you'll see how my words and
your understanding will form one strong truth.

"Everything in the world—things that die
and even things that can't die—reflect the
brilliance of the concept of the Holy Trinity:
God is the source of the Light, Jesus, who
was born of Him through contemplation and
introspection and who is as eternal and united
with Him as the Holy Spirit is. This light of God
is reflected down to Earth from the Heavens
through the prism of the nine orders of angels,
though its essence never changes. As it
descends down through the Spheres of
Paradise, it grows fainter and its power is
diminished, until finally it can produce only
secondary things. Or to put it more simply,
organic things and creatures of short lives.
But even so, the impression that it makes on
these creations is not absolute, and in each
one the light may shine more or less intensely.

"This is why trees of the exact same species
can produce different grades of fruit, and why
men are born with diverse and varied talents.
If each thing received the light perfectly, and

40

45

50

55

60

65

70

if Heaven's light wasn't diffused, then each
thing would shine with the light at full intensity.   75

"But nature is imperfect. She's more like
an artist who knows what he wants to
draw but whose hands are shaky.

"When the light of God shines brightest
and imprints the creation with its full   80
force, then perfection is achieved.
Such was Adam, formed from the
unspoiled earth of Eden, and such was the Son
conceived in the unspoiled womb of Mary.

"You can see now that you were right   85
to think that no humans could ever
match the wisdom of those two.
And if I left it at that, you'd still be
standing there pondering how it is that
I can say that 'Solomon is without equal.'   90

"But think about Solomon's request
when God asked him what he wanted:
He asked God to give him the wisdom
of a king so he could rule his people better.
He didn't ask for anything for himself. He   95
didn't ask how many angels there were
in Heaven, like Plato; and he didn't ask
about the philosophical premises that
Aristotle struggled with; or about the
mysteries of physics, or the perplexities   100
of geometry, or computer programming.
He didn't ask how to balance his checkbook!

"So when I talked about unmatched wisdom,
I was trying to make it clear that I was referring to
prudence, not book smarts or intellectual acrobatics.   105
If you remember, I used the word 'rose' when I
spoke about Solomon, which doesn't apply to Adam
or Jesus, since they were men who had no place to

CANTO XIII, 112—115: THOMAS'S HOMILY:

*"The whole point of this spiel of mine," he said,
"is mostly for you to see that sometimes you
have to just slow down and think about things
before you say 'yes' or 'no' to something."*

rise to. If you grasp what I'm saying in this sense, then
you'll see that it doesn't contradict what you believe   110
about Adam and Jesus being the wisest of all men.

"The whole point of this spiel of mine," he said,
"is mostly for you to see that sometimes you
have to just slow down and think about things
before you say 'yes' or 'no' to something. The   115
guy who rushes in to make judgments about
things before he knows anything about them is
pretty low on the list of fools. Oftentimes, hasty
and rash opinions can lead down the wrong
road and pride can get in the way of clear choices.   120

"Put it this way: It's no good heading off into
the world looking for truth unless you have
the skills to find it—otherwise, you're better
off staying home. George W. Bush is pretty
glaring proof of that! Or the philosophers   125
Parmenides, Bryson, and Melissus, who,
according to Aristotle, built their arguments on
erroneous assumptions. Or like Sabellius and
Arius and those who tried to deconstruct the Bible!

"So don't be too quick at making judgments.   130
Or, as they say, don't count your chickens
before they hatch. You might see the same
sidewalk covered in ice and snow all winter
long, but come spring a flower can still sprout
from between the cracks. And you can drive   135
all the way across the country safely, only to end
up having a wreck right in your own driveway.

"Don't be a know-it-all and think you've
got it figured out when you see one guy
giving money to the homeless and another   140
guy stealing. The generous one might
fail while the thief might be saved."

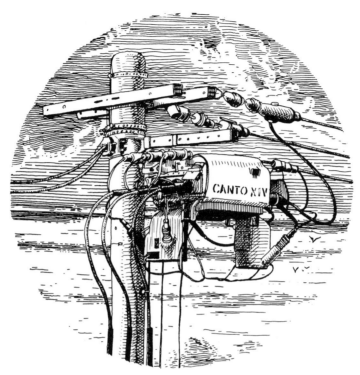

CANTO XIV

ARGUMENT

Still in the Fourth Heaven of the Sun, Beatrice asks the spirits to explain to Dante what will happen to them when the Resurrection of the Flesh arrives, the day of Final Judgment when all souls in Heaven will re-inhabit their Earthly bodies at the end of time. If you're put back into human forms, she asks, won't all this glowing light hurt your eyes? The spirit of Solomon, the wise king, answers, and explains that their refurbished bodies will be even better than they were in life. As he finishes, a third ring of lights appears distantly, but just then Dante and Beatrice are lifted up to the Fifth Heaven, the Sphere of Mars. There, two bands of lights appear in the form of a Cross and Dante has a vision of Christ. The souls sing in unison, a song more beautiful than anything he has heard until then.

Water in a round bucket will ripple
from the center outward, bouncing
back to the center again if it's bumped
on the outside or knocked from within.
This is the image that came to me in   5
that instant between the last words of
Thomas and the first of Beatrice, since
they seemed so similar. As he finished
she began speaking, politely, saying:

"He hasn't mentioned it yet—he hasn't yet   10
even formed the thought—but this man before
you needs to understand another truth down to
its roots. Please, explain to him whether or not the
resplendence in which you are now glowing will
stay with you forever; and if it will, then explain   15
to him how you will be able to stand to look at each
other without hurting your eyes, once you've got
your bodies back again on the final Judgment Day."

Like the thrilled, dancing crowd at a concert
that surges forward, renewed, faster, joining in   20
with the lyrics when one of their favorite songs
kicks in, those sparkling flames surged faster,
spinning, when they heard Beatrice's serious
and urgent demands for explanations.

People on Earth who think it's sad that we must all   25
die in order to reach eternal life have never seen the
glorious and refreshing showers of light that fall in Paradise.
The One and Two and Three at Once who rules in Heaven
and forever exists simultaneously as Three and Two and One,
containing all things and contained by nothing, was praised   30
in the songs of those rejoicing spirits three different times,
in such beautiful melodies that they went beyond anything
I have yet described. And then I heard a voice, which
sounded as sweet as the angel's must have when he
appeared to Mary, singing out from the brightest light of the   35
inner circle, the flame that burned with the spirit of Solomon.

"As long as our celebrations here in Paradise go
    on, our spirits will be wrapped in the glowing
    fire of our love you see now," he began.
"Its brilliance reflects our passion, our zeal   40
    reflects our sight, and it is measured by the
    grace we each merit. When we once again
    take on human forms, consecrated and
    glorified by our time spent up here, that flesh
    will be more beautiful and more complete   45
    than it was in our lifetimes. Then, any extra
    light that has been granted to us by the
    Highest Good will be enhanced, enabling
    us to see Him with Glorified eyes. And that
    light will make our own glow increase, burning   50
    brighter with our eagerness, our desire to see.

"Think of it as being like a piece of charcoal
    in a fire," he explained. "It glows brighter
    than the flames, but still holds its shape even
    in the hottest part of the fire. The glowing   55
    that you see surrounding us now will be outshone
    by our new bodies (which now lie buried
    in the Earth below). And the light won't tire us out,
    either, because our new bodies will come equipped
    with all the energy we'll need to enjoy them."   60

As he finished, the other spinning souls immediately
    sang out, "Amen!" and I could feel their eagerness
    to be back in their human bodies again—not just
    for themselves, I thought, but because they wanted
    to see their families again, their friends, all those   65
    whom they had loved before they became eternal flames.

And as I looked at them, I saw a new glow
    out beyond the two rings that circled us, as
    if the horizon was brightening at dawn.
    And at the same time it was like dusk,   70
    when the darkening sky starts to show new
    stars, distant and faint, so that at first you're
    not sure even if they're there or not. I thought

CANTO XIV, 103–106: THE VISION OF THE CROSS:

> And here's a point where my memory is better
> than my intellect, because I can't find any words
> to describe the flaming image of Christ that I saw
> glowing on that Cross.

I could see the lights of new spirits forming
a ring out beyond the two spinning wheels of lights.   75

A flash of radiance and a feeling of the Spirit's divine
love rushed and swirled around me, filling my eyes
and then seemed to drop away. When I glanced
at Beatrice beside me, she smiled and seemed
to glow even more beautiful in a way that I can't   80
really describe or even remember very well.

The sight of her gave me strength to pull myself
together and look up above. I saw that we were
rising again to a new level of Paradise, just the
two of us, and I knew that we were going up   85
because the warm glow of the planet of Mars
seemed to be redder than it usually is.

I closed my eyes, gave thanks, and offered
myself to God with all my heart, speaking to Him
through the universal language of love. I gave thanks   90
in proportion to this new level we had reached, and
even as this prayer was being formed in my heart
I could feel that it had already been accepted and
that it was pleasing. Two crimson rays appeared when
I opened my eyes, so bright and burning that, startled,   95
I said out loud: "Helios, this is what you look like?"

Imagine the band of the Milky Way as it stretches
from pole to pole across our sky, enticing astronomers
and perplexing philosophers. Those two rays I
saw there in the Sphere of Mars sparkled with   100
lights, intersecting and forming a Cross in front of
me, as if they were dividing a circle into four parts.

And here's a point where my memory is better
than my intellect, because I can't find any words
to describe the flaming image of Christ that I saw   105
glowing on that Cross. But anyone who accepts and
follows Christ himself will forgive me here for faltering
—seeing Him flash before me like that made me weak.

The lights sparkled and danced up
and down the Cross, from side to side,   110
passing and darting around, floating,
glittering as they went, some faster,
some slower, some shooting off at
an angle while others stood still. It was
like the particles of dust you see floating   115
around in a sunbeam as it pierces a dark
room through a drawn window shade.

The individual strings of a guitar or
a violin, each tuned to a different note,
when played together can speak to   120
your ears in a language without words.
Well, from those lights dancing before
me I heard a song that entranced me
with its melody. I could tell that it was
some kind of song of praise because I caught   125
the words "arise" and "We Shall Overcome,"
but I didn't catch much else. But it was
so enchanting, that song, that nothing
has ever held me like it did, so softly.

And what I'm writing here might seem presumptuous,   130
because for a moment you might be thinking that maybe
I thought the song was more beautiful and made me feel
better than Beatrice's peaceful gaze. But if you've been
paying attention you'll remember that I wrote that she became
more beautiful with every Sphere we reached, and you'll notice   135
that I hadn't looked at her yet there in Mars. So you'll forgive me,
just like I forgive myself, and you'll see that I'm being consistent
and telling the truth: I'm not saying she wasn't beautiful, what I'm
saying is that the higher we went the more perfect she became.

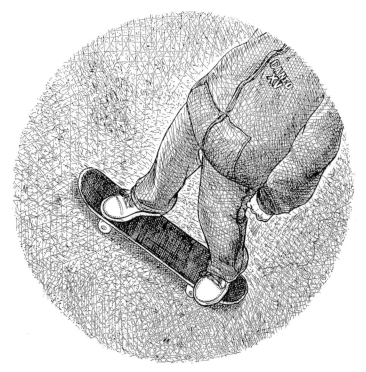

CANTO XV

ARGUMENT

As all the souls stop singing, Dante sees a star fall from the right side of the Cross all the way to the bottom. The light starts talking to him in very formal Latin, and then eventually chills out and relaxes a bit. The light says he understands why Dante doesn't ask his name or anything—because Dante knows these lights can see everything—but the light asks Dante to speak anyway, just because he likes the sound of Dante's voice. The light reveals himself to be Dante's great-great-grandfather, Cacciaguida, and he tells Dante that his great-grandfather is on the First Terrace of Purgatory. He then goes on to talk about how serene and peaceful and good Florence used to be, and finishes by describing his noble death during the Second Crusade.

True love always imparts good will, just
as greediness will result from selfish love.
Those souls that danced and sang before
me in that glittering instrument, played by
God's own hand, must have heard my prayers   5
and they answered with enthusiastic kindness.
How could anyone not see that all prayers will
be answered, when right in front of me they all
stopped singing and listened eagerly for my
questions? Nothing but sorrow waits for the man   10
who can't see this, and who turns his attention
instead to the temporary things of the world.

Sometimes when you're out on a clear
night staring at the stars you might see
a quick flash of light dart across the sky,   15
dragging your eyes with it as it goes,
before—in a second—it fades again into the
blackness, like fireworks on the Fourth
of July. As I stood there, one of those
sparkling souls shot toward the center   20
of the Cross like a meteor, then
shot down to the bottom, flaring up
brighter than all of the others as it went,
so that they seemed dim in comparison.

It darted as quickly as the soul of Anchises must   25
have done when he was reunited with his son
Aeneas in Elysian fields, as the great Virgil wrote.

"Oh blood of mine," it said, "What Heavenly grace
has been granted to you! To whom, like you, has
the gate of Paradise ever been opened twice?"   30

I heard that voice from the light and I stood
there amazed. Then I turned to look at Beatrice
for a clue, and that was even more disconcerting.
Her eyes were absolutely glowing with her smile,
and it seemed to me like I had just about   35
touched the essence of my own paradise.

And then the voice continued speaking from
that sparkling soul, but in his eagerness
everything he said was over my head. It was just
too deep and intense for me. He didn't do it on   40
purpose or anything, it was more like what he was
saying was just way too lofty for man to understand.

But after a minute he relaxed a bit. It was
as if love became a translator and he was
able to bring his thoughts down to layman's   45
terms. The first thing I understood was:
"Praise God, who is Three Beings in One and
who has been so kind to one of my own family!

"I have known that you were coming here for
a long time," he continued. "I have been   50
waiting for you, in fact, after seeing it foretold
in God's Big Black Book! It's good to see you, my
son, and my heart gives thanks to your girl there,
whose support enabled you to make this long trip.

"I know you're thinking that since I can read   55
your thoughts you don't have to ask me
who I am, or why I'm more excited to see
you than any of these other souls up here.
And you're right. Since I am closer to God,
and since everything in Paradise is united,   60
all of us up here, from the highest to the
lowest, are able to see thoughts reflected in
the Great Mirror, even before you think them!

"But please, even though God's sweet Light
fills me with eternal vision, I am still thirsty,   65
and one way this thirst can be quenched
is by actually hearing your voice. So go ahead,
ask your questions! Let your heart roam free—
I already know what you're going to ask."

I glanced over at Beatrice again, and she   70
knew what I was going to say even before
I said it. Her smile was enough for me.

CANTO XV, 88–91: IN THE FIFTH HEAVEN:

> "You're a branch of my own tree," he answered,
> "or rather, I am your root, and I was ecstatic when
> I heard that you were coming. I'm your great-great-
> grandfather, Cacciaguida."

"It's obvious to me, sir, that you're a very
intelligent and loving man," I said, "able
to see God's perfect balance around you.   75
And the Sun that both warms you with desire
and lights you with reason is set so perfectly
that there is no Earthly comparison. But as
you well know, humans are often unable to
express their needs, as our tongues and   80
hearts often speak very different languages.
As a man, I feel this disparity intensely, and
so I'm only able to thank you properly with my
heart and hope that my words are good enough.
And so I ask you, glowing topaz, beautiful   85
stone set within the ring of this beloved
jewel, please: tell me your name."

"You're a branch of my own tree," he answered,
"or rather, I am your root, and I was ecstatic when
I heard that you were coming. I'm your great-great-   90
grandfather, Cacciaguida. Your great-grandfather,
Alighiero, the one your family was named after, has
been circling around on the First Terrace of Purgatory
for a long time now. I am his father. If you get the
chance you might throw out a few prayers for him   95
down there and shorten his sentence, if you can.

"Our Florence was still enclosed in her ancient walls
and the church bells still rang at nine and three, but
it used to be a lot more peaceful than it is now. She
never dressed up in any tacky outfits in my day—   100
none of these gaudy necklaces or earrings, no showy
dresses or jewelry more flashy than the lovely woman
herself! Fathers didn't have to fear if they had a daughter
back then, because the age for marrying wasn't so
low and dowries weren't so high. There weren't any   105
of these gigantic, pretentious mansions you see now.
There were no families without kids, and Sardanapalus's
taste for luxury and lust hadn't infected our bedrooms.

"Florence's Mount Uccellatoio hadn't yet surpassed
Rome's Montemario, though it's since had a   110
faster rise and will have a harder fall, too.

"In those days, nobles like Bellincion Berti
    would walk around wearing nothing finer than
    leather and their wives would go out without
    makeup. Rich guys like dei Nerli and del Vecchio   115
    were happy wearing unlined suits and their
    wives didn't mind using a needle and thread.

"All wives were happy then," he went on.
"Their beds were always warm and shared;
    none of them worried about their husbands   120
    running off to do business in France. Wives would
    watch over the baby crib, cooing and gooing, the
    way all new parents do, and they'd be happy
    at the sewing machine and surrounded
    by kids who loved to hear the stories of   125
    the Trojans and of Rome and of Fiesole.

"The corrupt Lapo Salterello and the slutty Cianghella
    would've amazed the dutiful Florentines of old as much as
    the noble Cincinnatus or Cornelia would astonish them now.
    It was a serene and lovely place, full of content   130
    and productive citizens, all joined together in
    good faith and sweetness and light.

"Mary's name was called out when I was
    born, and I was baptized a Christian,
    and then given the name Cacciaguida.   135
    My brothers were Eliseo and Moronto
    and my wife came from the Po Valley,
    bringing the surname Alighiera with her.
    I served under the Emperor Conrad, who
    eventually knighted me in honor of my   140
    heroic service in the Second Crusade.
    He and I fought side by side against the backward
    laws of Islam, whose followers take over
    only because all the Popes were corrupt.

"It was there that I was killed and set free from   145
    the ties to the evil world, which waylay and bushwack
    so many hopeless souls. I died a martyr,
    and so I arrived in this eternal peace."

CANTO XVI

ARGUMENT

Still in the Fifth Heaven of Mars, Dante talks about pride in one's heritage and warmly questions Cacciaguida about what things were like in Florence when he was alive. Cacciaguida goes on a long discourse about the good old days—about when and where he was born, what the town was like, who were the important people around, and the rise and fall of a long list of important families in Florence.

It doesn't surprise me now that passions
for lineage and country can fill men's chests
with pride here on Earth where emotions are so much
less intense, because even up in Paradise—
where passions are steered toward more noble   5
loves and are so much stronger—even there I felt
a rush of pride inside me. But pride's a shirt that quickly
shrinks, as time tends to nip away at it around
the edges, unless you keep patching up the holes.

My first words to him were those of respect, that   10
form of "you" the Romans used only when
addressing Caesar (though they almost never use that form
anymore), and Beatrice smiled when she heard me
use it. It reminded me of when the Lady gave a little cough
to Guinevere to warn of her presence in the story of Lancelot.   15

"You are my father," I said to him.
"You embolden me to speak freely.
You lift me so that I am more than myself.
So many waves of happiness flood
my heart right now, it feels like   20
my mind is going to burst and overflow.
As the founder of my family, tell me about my
ancestors. When you were a boy, what
years made history back then? And what
was Florence like in those days, under its   25
patron, St. John? Was it a big place?
Who were the important people in town?"

Like the tip of a cigarette that glows brighter
with a drag, I saw the flame of old Cacciaguida
flare up a little brighter when he heard my words.   30
And even as I saw him more brilliantly, his
voice seemed to speak more kindly and
sweeter to me, with an accent of times past.

"Since the first *'Ave'* was spoken by the
angel to Mary until the day my mother (now   35
blessed in Heaven) gave birth to me," he answered,
"this star of Mars had circled five hundred
fifty-three times through the skies and the
constellation of Leo. My ancestors and I
were born within the old walls of Florence,   40
where the runner first comes into the district
where they hold the yearly horse race. But let's
not talk about them now—all that stuff about
who they were and where they came from—
it's better if we just leave that unsaid.   45

"Back when I was a kid, the whole population
of able-bodied men—from the statue of Mars on the
Ponte Vecchio to the Baptistery of San Giovanni
—was only a fifth of what it is now. But it was a
pure-blooded town down to the last man, not sullied   50
by those families from Campi, Certaldo, or Figline,
like it is today. It would be a lot better if they
were merely neighbors—if our borders didn't
reach beyond the towns of Galluzzo and Trespiano.
Now they're in our midst, and guys like   55
Aguglione and Signa hang around keeping a sharp eye
out for opportunities to bend things their way.

"If the Church had accepted Rome's
rule with motherly love, instead of with
the jealousy of a stepmother, then I know   60
one haggling merchant who would
have stayed home in Simifonti rather than
moving to Florence; the Conti Guidi family
would still be ruling at home in Montemurlo;
and the Cerchis would still be in Acone,   65
rather than stirring up trouble in our town.

"Whenever you bring people in from the
outside, it's bad for a town. It's like when
your belly's full but you just keep eating until
you're sick. Remember, the bigger they   70
come, the harder they fall; or maybe I
should say—too many cooks spoil the soup!

"Just think how the towns of Luni and
Urbisaglia, once thriving, are now in ruins.
And Sinigaglia and Chiusi are on their way   75
down the same path! If entire cities can go
to pot, it's no wonder that long-established
families can go downhill too.

"Men's deeds in life are as mortal as men
themselves, though it's not always evident,   80
as one's legacies can last longer than men's
short lives. But just as the forces of the Moon
cause the tides to rise and fall, hiding and
revealing the shoreline, so do the fortunes
of Florence ebb and flow. It should come as   85
no surprise to you to hear about families whose
reputations have been forgotten over the years.

"In my time," he went on, counting
off on his fingers, "I saw families like the
Ughis, the Catellinis, the Filippis, the Ormannis,   90
and the Alberichis all die off. On the other hand,
the Soldanieris were at their peak then,
along with the Bostichis, the L'Arcas,
the La Sannellas, and the Ardinghis.
The Ravignanis lived near the Porta San Pietro,   95
where the Cerchis live now with their boatload

of scandals that are about to take them down.
The Conti Guidis are descended from the
Ravignanis, as is the whole Bellincion clan.

"Oh, in those days," he continued, on a roll, "the   100
Della Pressa family was ruling things, and doing a
great job of it too, and the Galigaios had already been
knighted. The Pigli family, with their red-striped coat of arms,
were powerful back then, like the Giuochis, the Gallis, the
Baruccis, the Fifantis, the Sacchettis, and the Chiarmontesis,   105
even though one of them had embarrassed their name.

"The Calfucci boys were full grown by then, and the
Sizii and Arrigucci families were in office—this was
before they had to flee to Lucca, you see. There were
so many great names back then that have since been   110
dragged through the mud," he sighed. "Like the Ubertis
and the Lambertis, with their gold and blue crest.

"Even the Visdominis and the Tosinghis, who
lined their pockets when the bishop's seat
was empty, had good names back then. Those   115
bastards, the Adimaris, who bully around the
weak but cringe and cower in the corner whenever
anyone with any balls stands up to them, they
were even on the rise in those days—but they
had been so low-class to start with that old   120
Hubert Donato didn't want anything to do with them.

"Yep, the Caponsacchis had already moved
from Fiesole to that house by the Mercato Vecchio,
and the Giudi and Infangatos, they were around too.

"Oh, and you won't believe this!" he said, gaining   125
enthusiasm. "The old Della Pera family—who's
nothing nowadays—was so famous back in those
days that they even had a town gate named after them!
And those five families whose emblems all bear the
arms of Hugh the Great (whose anniversary of his death   130
is celebrated on St. Thomas's Day every year), they were
all knighted by him—although Giano della Bella's family
has since switched allegiances to the working class.

"The Gualterotti and Importuni families had
already moved into the Borgo neighborhood,   135
and if the Buondelmontis hadn't moved in too, it
would still be a nice area. The Amidei family—the
ones who started all the troubles when they killed
Buondelmonte (even though they had a good reason
to), they were respectable back then. Geez, that   140
Buondelmonte! If he hadn't listened to his buddy
and backed out of the wedding, things would be so much
different now! There're plenty of people who wish he
(along with anyone who starts a stupid war) would have
just jumped off a bridge into the river and drowned, but it   145
was Florence's fate to be the place of his murder—right
there at the very statue of Mars, no less, on the Ponte Vecchio!

"Yeah," he exhaled, remembering. "Those
were the families of Florence back in my day.
Things were good back then. That was back   150
when the city's logo was still the white lily on
the red background, before the Guelf party
came along and reversed it, before that lily had
been bloodied by the divisions yet to come."

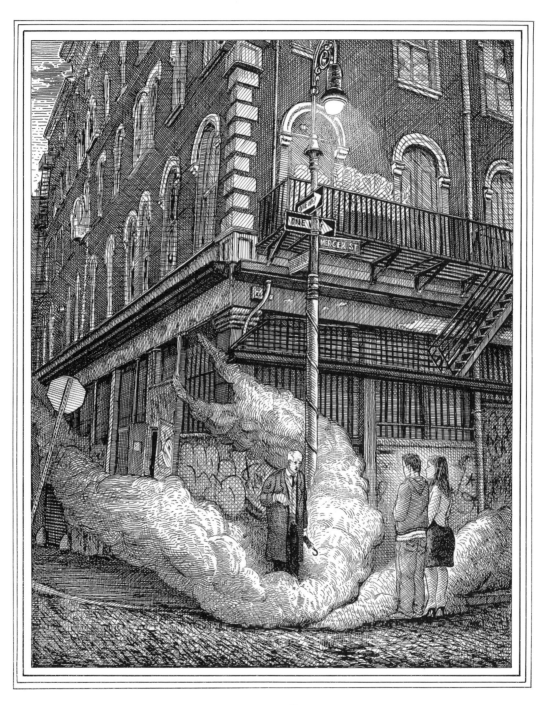

CANTO XVI, 148–150: CACCIAGUIDA:

> "Yeah," he exhaled, remembering. "Those
> were the families of Florence back in my day.
> Things were good back then."

CANTO XVII

ARGUMENT

Still in the Sphere of Mars, both Beatrice and Cacciaguida know what Dante's question will be and urge him to ask quickly as he won't be in Paradise for much longer. Dante says that he'd heard rumors about his future and asks his great-great-grandfather to explain the truth behind what he's heard. Cacciaguida tells Dante that in the future he will be exiled from Florence with his White Party, but that Bartolommeo della Scala, a lord in Verona, will take him in and become his friend. There Dante will meet Bartolommeo's young brother, Can Grande, who is destined to become a great military leader (and to whom Dante dedicated his Paradiso*). Dante then wonders whether he should be brutally honest about what he has seen in the afterlife when he writes about it in his poem, and Cacciaguida tells him that he must, as his writing will be important to the world. He tells him that writing about the famous people he's met is the way people will most believe him, since the examples of known people leave readers with some reference point to judge them.*

S tanding there, I felt like Phaeton must've
felt when he heard all the rumors that he wasn't
really Apollo's son and he went to his mom,
Clymene, for answers. I'd heard all kinds of predictions
in the other Spheres and now I appealed to   5
Beatrice and Cacciaguida to tell me the truth.

"Now is the time for you to ask about anything
   that's bothering you," Beatrice said to me,
"even your deepest concerns. Not that we
   need to hear you say it, but it's better for   10
you to learn how best to speak for yourself
   so your doubts can be properly satisfied."

"My dear and wise great-great-grandfather," I said,
"men are able to see and understand Earthly
   problems like geometry in simple truths. But   15
you, up here near that Point where all time is
   eternal, you are able to see the infinite, you can
see events even before they come to pass.

"Back when I was traveling with Virgil, climbing
   up Mt. Purgatory where souls are cleansed as well as   20
running around through the fires of the Inferno
below, I heard some pretty ominous predictions
   about me, some nasty rumors. Not that I feel
vulnerable to the random blows of chance or anything;
   but still, I'm kinda dying to know what the future   25
really has in store for me. If you know where
   the bullet's coming from, you have time to duck."

That's how I put it when I spoke to
   Cacciaguida. I had asked my question,
just like Beatrice wanted me to. And he   30
answered me plain and simple, too, not
   with any of the twisted logic or confusing
metaphors that used to trip up fools
   back in the old days, but with straight-up
explanations. And though he was hidden   35
   by the glow, his smile revealed his pleasure.

"Even the incidental events of the material
world are known by us up here in Paradise,"
he said. "But knowing about things that will
happen doesn't mean that we cause them   40
to happen, any more than a plane taking off
is powered by you watching it go.

"The events of the future, what's in store
for you in your life ahead, come to me
like a song in my head. I can tell you that,   45
just like Hippolytus who was exiled from
Athens by his conniving and lying stepmother,
you are going to be forced to leave Florence.
This is a done deal, already being planned
and set into motion by Pope Boniface VIII,   50
who rules where religion can be bought and
sold. As usual, most people are going to
blame the victim, but just vengeance will
punish the guilty ones in the long run.

"You are going to have to leave behind   55
everything you care about most in life—
that will be the first blow. And you will learn
what it's like to walk in others' shoes, what it's
like to eat humble pie, and how hard life can
be when you have to follow others' footsteps.   60

"But worst of all for you will be the
useless scheming of your fellow
exiles in the White Party. They're a
bunch of crazy, thankless backstabbers
and they'll turn against you down the line,   65
although soon after they do they'll regret
it. Their ineffectualness will be obvious
in their deeds, and you'll be better off
being a party of one than with them.

"Eventually you'll find refuge in Verona,   70
with the great Lombard lord whose seal
is the eagle above the golden ladder.

CANTO XVII, 43–45: CACCIAGUIDA'S PREDICTIONS:
"The events of the future, what's in store
for you in your life ahead, come to me
like a song in my head."

He'll take you in with respect, and his
generosity and friendship will be such
that you won't have to ask for anything.   75

"And there you'll be fortunate enough
to meet his younger brother, Can Grande.
Born under the sign of this planet, Mars,
he is destined for greatness, although
the world hasn't noticed him yet because   80
he's still young—the planets have only been
circling him for nine years so far. But even
before Pope Clement V betrays Emperor
Henry VII, this young one will be showing
signs of distinction through hard work and   85
scorn of wealth. His generosity will be hard
for even his enemies to ignore. Keep an eye
on him; expect great things. His influence
will bring many changes to society—the
rich will become poor, and beggars rich.   90

"Now listen closely to what I'm going to tell you,
but keep it locked up in that head of yours," he said.
Then he went on to describe the future deeds of
Can Grande della Scala, things so amazing that
they will surprise even those that live to see them.   95

"These are the truths of what you've heard before.
These are the traps that await you," he concluded.
"But don't envy your neighbors. Your life will far
exceed the punishments of their betrayals."

And with that Cacciaguida was silent, having   100
finished weaving the tapestry of my future
over the fabric of all my fears and insecurities.

I stood there thinking, and, like anyone
who has doubts and turns to someone
wise who they can trust for advice, I said: 105

"I have to thank you, Father. I can see now
how quickly I'm heading for a fall that would

be way worse if you hadn't warned me of it.
Your words give me some time to prepare so
that even if I have to lose Florence, maybe my   110
poem might still affect the places I pass through.

"On this whole journey I've been making—down
through Hell and eternal damnation, then all the
way up Mt. Purgatory to where I met Beatrice here,
who has guided me up through these Heavens,   115
floating from light to light—I've seen all kinds of
things that will piss a lot of people off if I call it
how I saw it. But then again, if I don't write about
everything just how it is, then I'm afraid I'll just be
lost in the sea of history to those who come after me."   120

As I was talking I saw the glow around my
great-great-grandfather flashed brighter,
like a windshield reflecting the summer Sun.

"The only people who aren't going to like
what you have to say are those who have   125
something to hide," he said. "You shouldn't
go easy on them, you should write about
what you've seen and let those who are
bothered by it deal with it however they want.

"Like a lot of things that are good for you, what   130
you write might seem bitter and take some
getting used to at first. Your poem might even
stir up a windstorm of controversy, ruffling the
edges of Popes and politicians with your honesty.

"And as you've learned everywhere you've been—   135
down in Hell, up on Purgatory, or even here in Paradise—
it's the famous people you write about who are
the best examples for your readers, because they
won't believe what you have to say if they've never
heard of the people you're talking about. They won't   140
have any reference to judge them by, and your
arguments and examples won't be meaningful."

CANTO XVIII

ARGUMENT

Dante ponders Cacciaguida's dire predictions about his future, but Beatrice reassures him. Then Cacciaguida names the other eight souls who are with him in the Fifth Sphere of Mars, each one an example of strength and fortitude. As they are named, they flash around in the Cross of stars. Dante turns to Beatrice and sees her growing yet more beautiful and then realizes that they have risen to the next Heaven, the Sphere of Jupiter. There, the lights of souls appear in clusters before them, forming letters that spell out, in Latin, the first sentence from Solomon's Book of Wisdom: *"Love justice, ye that judge the Earth." The letters appear one by one in Gothic script and when they form the last "M" they hover in formation. Another swirl of lights appears and gathers at the top of the "M," forming a flower, and then all the lights rearrange themselves into the image of an eagle. This vision leads Dante into a rant against the Church in Rome, led astray by Pope John XXII, whom he accuses of being more interested in making a profit than in ministering to his flock.*

With that, the Heavenly gleam fell silent, seeming
to contemplate what he had just said, and so
did I, pondering the good news and the bad.
Then Beatrice, my guide on the path to God, said,
"Look at it this way: Remember that I'm in with   5
the Guy who can make *anything* easier to bear."

The kindness her voice carried
made me turn toward her, but I'm
not even going to try to write about the
love I saw in her eyes. It's not just that   10
I doubt I can ever capture it in words,
I don't think I can *even* remember
it well enough, unless Someone were
to help me. The only thing I can say for
sure is that when I looked at her, I felt   15
there was nothing more in life I needed,
nothing lacking inside my very soul—
as long as she looked at me with those eyes.

She smiled at me and I went weak.
"You should give *Him* your attention," she said.   20
"There's more to Paradise than just my eyes."

Sometimes someone here on Earth is so
overcome by an emotion that they forget
themselves and you can see everything they're
feeling in their expression. When I turned back to   25
the burning soul of Cacciaguida I could plainly
see that he was dying to say something else.

"In this Fifth Sphere of Heaven," he began, "the Tree
of Paradise grows in reverse, down from its source,
and it is always full of fruit and never loses its leaves.   30
On it are the blessed souls of those who were so
famous in life that any poem with them in it would be
the better for it. Before you go, take a good look at
the Cross and let me name some of the souls who
sparkle within it. Watch and you'll see   35
them dance like lightning as I name them."

With that, he spoke the name of Joshua
and I saw a flash shoot along the Cross
and it was gone in an instant. At the name
of Maccabee another light whipped   40
around the arms of that constellation,
spinning like a top spun by happiness.

Then Charlemagne, and the gleam of
Roland took off after it, and I watched them both
glide like you watch the arch of your own free throw.   45

William and Renouard flashed along the
Cross, drawing my eyes, followed by Duke
Godfrey and Robert Guiscard. After that,
old Cacciaguida drifted away to mingle
with the others, joining in their songs   50
and showing off his extraordinary voice.

I turned to Beatrice on my right,
hoping she'd tell me or motion
what I should do next, and her
eyes were shining so clearly and   55
so full of bliss that again they
surpassed anything I'd ever seen.

I had a feeling like when you've made a big
decision and are working toward something,
when each day you're more sure you're doing   60
the right thing, improving, more confident, and
I noticed that our revolutions seemed to have
expanded, that her beauty had increased even more.

Turning around I noticed that the reddish
glow of Mars had faded to the pale,   65
balmy white of the Sixth Heaven, faded
softly like the flush of embarrassment
that drains from the cheeks of a pale girl
once the moment has passed.

CANTO XVIII, 70–73: IN THE SIXTH HEAVEN OF JUPITER:
The lights
danced around us, sparkling with love,
and gathering until they formed the letters
of words.

DANTE'S PARADISO

In that Heaven of Jupiter, the lights   70
danced around us, sparkling with love,
and gathering until they formed the letters
of words. It was like a flock of seagulls on
the beach that rises up in a mass when
startled, squawking and forming a ball or a   75
cloud or some other shape. The floating souls
swarmed around us, singing, and formed the
letter "D," then an "I," and then an "L." At first
it seemed that they flowed to the beat of
their song, but as they formed each letter   80
they paused for a moment in silence.

And here again I must call on the gifts of
the Muses to aid me, gathered where they
are around Pegasus's fountain. May your
light guide me as I search in the dark   85
for the words to describe those signs
as I see them etched in my memory.

As we watched, those Heavenly spirits
formed thirty-five letters before us,
and I spelled out the words as they appeared.   90
"DILIGITE IUSTITIAM" were the first verb
and noun that appeared in that display,
followed by "QUI IUDICATIS TERRAM."
And with the last "M" they stopped, suspended,
glowing brightly so that the silver mists of the   95
Heaven of Jupiter seemed to be infused with gold.

Soon another crowd of lights came down and
gathered at the top of the letter. As they came
they sang in praise of the Good that drew them
together, as near as I could guess. And then a   100
thousand lights seemed to rise up in a rush,
some fast, some slow, apparently toward some
predetermined formation. It was like when you
toss an empty beer bottle into a campfire and it
kicks up a shower of sparks that rise from the coals.   105
And all the lights settled into place above that

glittering letter until they formed the image of a
flower above it. Then gradually all the lights
began to move, like the flakes in a plastic snow
globe, until they had formed into the head of an   110
eagle, and the arms of the "M" became its wings.

In those visions, the artistry of the One who
made them was obvious. He copies no one,
He creates Himself, shaping the forces as they flow.

Those sparkling, innumerable stars   115
that I saw in the Sphere of Jupiter
demonstrated the Earthly justice that
they embody. And in my head I asked
that He who moves them pay attention
to the smoke that is darkening the skies   120
over Rome, dimming Jupiter's glow.
I asked that He punish those Popes
responsible for leading the Church
down the wrong road, and I prayed for the
souls of those who had followed down   125
that path. Wars used to be fought with
weapons, and those Popes are now using
the sacraments themselves as a weapon
instead of as the nourishment they should be.

But you especially, John XXII, may you   130
not forget that the eyes of Peter and Paul—
who died for the Church you're ruining—
are watching you! And I bet you'd say:

"I work for St. John the Baptist, whose face
adorns our coins. I don't think I know this   135
Paul or this Fisherman you're referring to."

CANTO XIX

ARGUMENT

The image of the eagle, formed by the lights of the souls of just kings and politicians, speaks with one voice, telling Dante that it is the symbol of Divine Justice. Dante wants to better understand the nature of Justice, but the Eagle explains that it is a concept beyond human understanding, that the workings of God's deeds must, by definition, be beyond the comprehension of His creations. The Eagle explains that the Bible is proof of this and that it should be a guiding light for humankind. Dante then asks about what happens to the virtuous souls who lived before Jesus Christ and therefore couldn't be Christians, or who lived in distant places and never heard of Jesus. The Eagle replies that some of these souls are closer to God on Judgment Day than hypocritical Christians might be, and ends with a rant against the hypocritical and evil rulers of Dante's time.

The image of that Eagle hung in the
air in front of me, its wings spread
wide, filled with the sparkling, flickering
lights of the hundreds of souls that
flashed inside it like the neon lights in   5
the marquee of a Las Vegas casino.

And what I'm going to tell you now
has never been written about or
made into a movie scene ever before:
The beak of that Eagle moved up and   10
down like it was talking, even though
it was made up of tons of different lights.

"Justice and mercy were the keys to my rule,"
its voice said, "and that is why you see me
here in the Sphere of Jupiter. This is where   15
I belong. The legacy I left on Earth is
so honored that even evil men give it lip service,
even if they refuse to follow my example."

And just as one heat rises from the many coals
in a barbeque, one voice came from that Eagle   20
even though it was made up of many souls.

"Dear souls, sparkling up here in the
garden of your eternal happiness like
flowers in a garden whose scents rise
together into one smell," I said, "please,   25
can you answer some of the questions that have
been bugging me for years down on Earth?
I understand that the foundations of God's
Justice are actually located in a higher Sphere
above, but that all of you here in this ring see its   30
workings clearly. You also know how keen
I am to learn and you know the nature of the
question that's been bugging me for so long."

When a teenage girl realizes that a cute guy
nearby is looking at her she gets self-conscious   35

CANTO XIX, 1–4: THE VISION OF THE EAGLE:
*The image of that Eagle hung in the
air in front of me, its wings spread
wide, filled with the sparkling, flickering
lights of the hundreds of souls.*

and proud, straightening her outfit and glowing
with confidence. That's how that Eagle seemed
when it sensed my questions, with all the
souls singing together in praise of Paradise.

"God is infinite and the architect of   40
order from chaos," the Eagle began. "It
should be obvious that no finite thing that
He creates can possibly understand the
workings of His ideas, His Justice. As proof,
think how His most perfect creations are the   45
Angels. Lucifer was the most perfect of all
of them, God's brightest angel. But he fell from
Paradise because he was too impatient to wait
for Divine Grace. If Lucifer was that close to
God and was unable to reach perfection, just   50
think how far all the other creatures are from it.

"Think about it: our intelligence is itself
created by God, and it's a reflection
of Him. Therefore it is incapable of
understanding God beyond what God   55
decides to show us of Himself. The
intellectual vision of mankind can no
more understand God's will and justice
than see to the bottom of the sea.
Now of course you can see the sandy   60
bottom near the shore, but you can't
see it out in the middle of the ocean.
Even though it's there, it's way too deep to see.

"The intellect of the soul is constantly shadowed
by the faults of the body—the desires of the flesh,   65
the stains of sin. Only the pure light of God can
illuminate it. And now you should see where the
answers to your questions have been hiding.

"And I can see your next question," the Eagle continued.
"'What about a man who's born someplace   70
like India?' you're thinking, 'a place where
there's no one to teach him about Jesus? And
let's say that man is good and fair, and that, as

far as anyone can see, he lives a perfectly
virtuous life. And let's say he dies unbaptized.   75
How can it be just that his soul is condemned?
How has he sinned if he doesn't know any better?'

"But hold on a second," the Eagle went on.
"Who are you to judge things a thousand miles away
when you can barely see beyond your own nose?   80
Perhaps if we didn't have the Bible to guide us,
some people could argue the finer points of God's
will—but everything's right there in the Book for you!

"O creatures down below on Earth, get this into
your thick skulls: God's will is always good, and it   85
never strays from Itself and always follows Truth.
All things in line with God's will are just and fair.
It's not concerned with what's fashionably fine,
but creates good by shining throughout the world."

You know how pigeons feed their chicks in   90
rooftop nests, then fly around the building while
the baby that was fed peeks over the fire escape
to watch? That sacred Eagle, glittering with the
lights of all those souls, circled around me like a
mother bird, and I stood there, content, watching it.   95

And as it circled the souls sang: *"My notes*
are too high for you to understand,
just as Eternal Judgment is to mankind."

Finally that whole constellation of lights
stopped singing and, still in the form of an   100
eagle of the Roman Empire, it said: "No one
who does not believe in Christ has ever risen
to Paradise. Not in the days before He was
crucified or after. Even so, there are many
who say they worship Him today that will be   105
farther from Him on the Final Judgment
than many who have never heard of Him.
Even the innocent pagans will condemn
these so-called Christians on Judgment Day,
when it's obvious who is saved and who is not.   110

"What do you think the Muslims and Buddhists
and Hindus will say to the corrupt kings when
they see God's book of judgment? Clearly written
will be the deeds of the usurper Emperor Albert
of Austria, who will invade and destroy   115
Prague out of jealousy. They will read about
the economic ruin of France, wrought by
Philip the Fair who will devalue their money
to pay for his wars, and who will be killed by
a wild boar. They will clearly see the selfish   120
pride that infects both Longshanks and Braveheart,
neither of whom is happy to stay within their bounds.

"Written for all to see will be the perverted,
lazy lives of King Ferdinand of Spain
and of Wenceslaus IV, king of Bohemia.   125
The book, keeping score, counts exactly *one*
virtue for Charles II of Naples, cripple of Jerusalem,
and at least *one thousand* of his perversities.

"Written in that book will be the greed and
cowardice of Frederick II, sent to guard the   130
Island of Sicily where Anchises died. There
will be notes in the margins and tiny letters
used there, to squeeze all of his errors and
blunders onto the pages allowed. And all the
horrific deeds of his brother James II and of his   135
uncle James in their kingdoms of Mallorca and
Aragon will be described in the book as well.

"Norway's King Haakon V, Portugal's King Diniz,
and Serbia's King Stephen Urosh II, who counterfeits
Italian coins, will all be laid bare in those pages.   140

"Hungary would be happy if she was
left alone, and Navarre would be safer
if the Pyrenees were better protection.
Her fate can be seen in the example of the
towns of Nicosia and Famagosta on Cyprus,   145
conquered by the Frenchman Henry II, whose own
evil deeds deserve his listing with the others there."

CANTO XX

ARGUMENT

In the Sixth Heaven, the Eagle speaks about the souls there in the Sphere of Jupiter, the Sphere of Justice. It introduces six glowing souls who make up the eye and brow of the image, those who led the most exemplary lives of justice on Earth. They include King David; the Roman Emperors Constantine and Trajan; William II, King of Naples and Apulia; and Ripheus, a hero of Troy from Virgil's book the Aeneid. Dante is amazed to see Trajan and Ripheus in Heaven, as they lived before Christ and so could not have become Christians and should now be in Limbo with Virgil. Before he can ask about it the Eagle answers, explaining that Trajan was resurrected through prayer and converted, and that Ripheus was given a glimpse of the future by God and was baptized by the three women whom Dante met in the Garden of Eden. The workings of God can never be understood by man, the Eagle warns. They might not make sense all the time, but that's just the way it is.

At the end of the day, the Sun, which
lights our world, settles so low beyond
the horizon that the Earth grows dark.
Almost immediately the sky is lit again
by the sparkle of millions of stars,   5
where only one Sun had shown before.

I thought about that celestial transformation
from one to many as the Eagle, that
symbol of the world, went silent. But even
as it did the souls making up its form   10
seemed to sparkle ever faster, singing
songs so pleasant they escape me now.
The notes they sang rang out with sweet
melodies of pure love, fervently sung,
inspired by nothing but the Divine.   15

Pretty soon all those glittering, singing souls
that reside up there in the Heaven of Jupiter
finished their song and went quiet. And then
I heard a sound like the murmur of a
creek in the mountains—soft and pleasant—   20
that implies a deeper, more abundant source.
This sound seemed to come from inside
the crowd of lights that formed the symbol,
and it rose up through them like a crowd
doing the wave at a baseball game, or maybe   25
more like breath through a saxophone that
carries the notes along with it as it goes.
And that soft song became a stream that rose
up through the mouth of the Eagle and became
a voice that touched me to my very heart.   30

"Pay attention now and look carefully,"
that voice began. "Watch that place
around my eye, which in mortal eagles
can see and feel the rays of the Sun.
Of all the souls that comprise me, the   35
six most important ones are found there.

"In the very center, like a pupil, sparkles the
soul of David, who carried the Ark of the
Covenant from Gibeah to Gath to Jerusalem.
When he wrote the Psalms, the Holy Spirit and his   40
own spirit moved him. Here he has learned the
rewards of those whose will works with His will.

"In my brow, the light closest to my beak is
Emperor Trajan, who paused on his march
to console a grieving widow. Here he has   45
learned the rewards of service to Christ,
even as he learned its consequences
in the time he spent below, in Limbo.

"The light next to his on my brow is that
of Hezekiah, King of Judah. When his time   50
had come on Earth he prayed for more
and was granted fifteen extra years of life.
Here he has learned that holy judgment
cannot be avoided, only delayed.

"The brightest light at the peak of my brow   55
is Emperor Constantine, who moved the
government and the eagle standard from
Rome to Byzantium. Here he has learned
that though the results of his good acts
were ruinous, they are not held against him.   60

"The next light along is King William
the Good, whose lands have since
suffered under the rule of Charles II
and Frederick II. Here he has learned
that Heaven loves a just leader, and   65
he sparkles now with those rewards.

"And who down below would ever
believe it if you told them that the fifth
light was Ripheus of Troy? Here he
has learned much more than mortals   70
about Divine Justice, although he'll
never grasp its deepest traits."

CANTO XX, 81–83: DANTE BEFORE THE EAGLE:

*I couldn't contain myself and the sentence
"Are you kidding me?" burst out before
I could stop it.*

With that the Eagle was silent, like
a chirping bird who, having flown and
sung, seems pleased with himself and   75
sits silently preening. That Heavenly
symbol of the Justice who molds all things
to what they are floated before me, glittering.
And even though my amazement must've been
crystal clear to them in my expression,   80
I couldn't contain myself and the sentence
"Are you kidding me?" burst out before
I could stop it, setting off a riot of sparkles,
like laughter, in the display before me.

And that sacred symbol, its eye even more   85
brilliant, answered so that I wouldn't be
left standing there with my mouth open.

"Since you're addressing them here, I'm sure
you know you're not being fooled. What you
mean to ask is, rather, 'How can this be possible?'   90
You're like a schoolboy who knows all the names
of cars but has no comprehension of their
complexities and needs to have them explained.

"As you see, the Kingdom of Heaven is a
party and *can* be crashed by those not invited,   95
but only if their hearts are full of boundless hope
and burning love. But rather than being a
defeat of God's will, these exceptions are
instead Divine victories. He welcomes them.

"You're astonished to see Trajan and   100
Ripheus sparkling away near my eye.
But despite what you thought, at the moments
of their deaths they were not pagans but
were, in fact, Christians. Even though one
died after Christ's Crucifixion and the other before   105
He was even born, both died with their faith secure.

"Trajan there came back from Limbo
to re-inhabit his old bones, even
though no one ever gets out of that place.
But the living St. Gregory had burning   110

hope for him, and his prayers for Trajan's
resurrection were answered. Once he was
alive again, this glowing soul you see
here was so quick to convert and so
earnest in his devotion that at his second   115
death he was judged worthy of coming
up here to join our celebrations.

"Old Ripheus here came by a different
route, thanks to a bottomless grace that
gushes from the deepest of hidden springs.   120
In life he lived decently and virtuously,
and in reward God gave him a glimpse
of the redemption that was yet to come
through Jesus. In that way he had a faith
in Christ even in pagan times, and told   125
all around him of their errors. So even a thousand
years before St. John was ever baptizing
people, those three sisters Faith, Hope, and Love
you met by the chariot in Eden baptized him.

"The roots of predestination are a   130
long way off for those who can't see
the bigger tree right in front of them.

"And so all men must be careful when they
judge each other. Even though we souls up
here have seen God Himself, we have no   135
clue who's on his list to be saved or anything.
But not knowing is fine by us. We're happy when
He's happy, whatever He wants, we want too."

And with those words from that symbol, drawn
in Paradise by God's own hand, I saw that I had   140
misunderstood some things up until then. Now
they were all cleared up. And I remember clearly
that while the Eagle had been speaking the lights
of those two great souls contained inside it
had been blinking on and off together as   145
he spoke, in affirmation, it seemed, and
in unison to its words, like the notes from
a piano that join with the voice of a singer.

CANTO XXI

ARGUMENT

Beatrice and Dante ascend into the Seventh Sphere of Saturn, the Sphere of contemplative souls. Beatrice can't smile, she explains, because her smile would blind him with its brilliance this high up in Heaven. Dante sees an enormous, golden ladder stretching up into space with the lights of souls descending it. A glowing soul approaches and Dante speaks to it, asking who it is and why it is quiet in this part of Paradise. The soul is that of Peter Damian, who explains that he was predestined to speak with Dante, but that to understand this is beyond Dante's ability. He talks about his past in a monastery and as a cardinal, then rants about the greediness and overindulgences of the Church. His tirade attracts a crowd of souls, who surround them and give out a loud shout.

By now I was staring at Beatrice again,
my eyes locked on her face and my mind
unable to think of anything else in the world.

She didn't smile back at me, but said,
"If I were to smile at you now, you'd   5
suffer the same fate of Semele, who
was turned to ashes when she was
faced with Jupiter's full divinity. You've
already noticed that my beauty gets more
intense with each Sphere we visit.   10
If I didn't shade you from it, my brilliance
would be like a bolt of lightning to your brain.

"If you notice, we have now arrived at Saturn,
the Seventh Sphere, under the sign of Leo
in the Heavens, whose rays carry his strength   15
as they shine on Earth below. Now let your
thoughts follow your eyes and let your eyes
be mirrors for the one you will meet here."

If you were able to understand the
joy I felt as I stood there staring   20
at Beatrice, then you might be able
to grasp how obeying her wishes
to turn away from her was just as
pleasing as seeing her beautiful face.

The ancient times of the poets was   25
known as the Golden Age, the Reign
of Saturn, and as I looked around inside
that Sphere I saw an enormous, golden
ladder, glittering as it reflected the sunlight,
rising up into the sky until it was lost in   30
the haze. And there were so many lights
coming down the ladder that it looked
like headlights on a freeway at rush hour.

In the city, commuters funnel out of a train
station like a flock in the morning; some   35

CANTO XXI, 28–31: THE LADDER OF PERFECTION:
I saw an enormous, golden
ladder, glittering as it reflected the sunlight,
rising up into the sky until it was lost in
the haze.

head uptown, some downtown, some flag
a cab and speed off to who knows where,
while some only have to cross the street
to work, and others linger around the station
talking on cell phones. The souls on that   40
ladder were like that, bunching up and swirling
around, then heading off in different directions.

As I watched, one of the lights nearest to
us seemed to shine so brightly that I thought
to myself, "You seem to be glowing so much   45
that I wonder who you are. But since Beatrice
isn't saying anything I should keep my mouth
shut, even though I'm dying to ask you about it."

Of course Beatrice knew exactly what I
was thinking. "Go ahead," she said, turning   50
toward me, "ask him whatever you want."

"Excuse me kind soul, gleaming there in
your happiness," I said. "I hate to bother
you, and if not for me, then for the sake
of my lovely Beatrice here, but could I trouble   55
you with a couple of questions? Could
I ask who you are and why you came over
to us? And can you tell me why everyone is
so quiet up here, when the other places
we've been everyone is singing all the time?"   60

"No one here is singing because of you,"
he answered politely, "for the same reason
Beatrice doesn't smile. Your mortal ears,
like your mortal eyes, wouldn't be able to
stand the intensity of our songs. When I saw   65
you as I was coming down the stairs I came
over to welcome you simply because it was
willed from above, not because I am any
friendlier than these other souls around here.
God's will, which guides us toward wisdom   70
and goodness in the world, gives us
each a mission in life, as you now see."

"I understand that true freedom
consists in submission to God's will,"
I said. "But what I don't understand   75
is why, of all the people around here,
you would be singled out to talk to
me, even if He directed it from above."

Even before I got the last word out,
that guy started spinning around like   80
mad, sparkling like a hubcap in the sun.

"The light of God shines down on me," the
voice from that gleam replied. "It penetrates
my soul, and wraps me in this light, filling
my eyes with His power and lifting me   85
beyond myself until I can see the Primal
Source itself. It's this sensation and
connection that fuels my inner fire, burning
with the clarity of understanding it brings.

"But even the most enlightened soul in   90
all the Spheres of Heaven couldn't answer
the question you just asked. The answer
that you're looking for is so buried in the
mysteries of Eternal Law that it's beyond
the understanding of every human.   95

"And you should tell that to everyone on Earth
when you get back there, so that they don't
keep wasting their time trying to figure it out.
Down there the brain is slow and dull, not
sharp and clear like up here. Think about it: 100
how can humans figure out something that is
beyond comprehension even in Paradise itself?"

Needless to say, I shelved the whole predestiny
question after his little speech and decided to just
ask his name—as humbly as possible.   105

"Between the Adriatic and Tyrrhenian seas—
not far from your hometown—there's a mountain
range called the Apennines," he answered in his

long-winded fashion. "There's a ridge that stretches
between them called Catria, and below that lies   110
the monastery of Santa Croce di Fonte Avellana.

"I spent two years studying there,
so diligent in God's service that
I survived on only bland vegan food
and water, freezing in wintertime and   115
sweating in summer, taking refuge only
in contemplative thinking. That monastery
used to produce all kinds of souls who
ended up in Heaven, but has since become
so empty its weakness will be revealed.   120

"My name is Peter Damian, and I called myself
Peter the Sinner over in the monastery of
Santa Maria in Porto, along the Adriatic's shore.
I was getting on in life when I was chosen
to become a cardinal, forced to wear that hat   125
that seems to get more corrupt all the time.

"In the old days, guys like Saints Peter and
Paul led the church, dedicated to preaching,
wandering the world in poverty, and accepting
whatever food was offered. But priests   130
nowadays are so fat that they need help just
getting out of their chairs. They're so fat that
their robes are like muumuus, and who knows
what's going on underneath them! Geez, who
would have thought it would ever come to this!"   135

As he spoke I saw tons of lights coming down the
ladder, almost as if his speech was riling them up.
They spun around and sparkled beautifully as they
came, and they gathered around us and stopped,
and suddenly they gave out a shout I could never   140
explain. But whatever they said was beyond me, and
it was so loud in that silence that it left me astounded.

CANTO XXII

ARGUMENT

The angry shout of the souls startles Dante, but Beatrice reminds him that he's in Paradise, where nothing bad can happen. The sparkling soul of St. Benedict, founder of the Benedictine Order and proponent of monastic life, now comes forward and introduces himself and others who represent the contemplative life: Romualdus and St. Macarius. The poet asks St. Benedict if he'll turn down his glow so that Dante can see his face, but Benedict says that the time for that will come later in the final Heaven, where all desires are satisfied. The way to reach it, he explains, is up Jacob's ladder, which Dante can see rising up into the sky. The souls whip away in a whirlwind, and in an instant Dante has flown up the ladder with Beatrice to the Eighth Sphere, the Heaven of the Fixed Stars. They pause and Beatrice tells Dante to look down and see how far they have come. Beyond all of the seven Heavens below them, Dante can see the Earth, tiny and insignificant.

Their shout startled and amazed me so
much that I turned back to Beatrice like a
toddler who hides behind his mother's legs.
And like a mother who speaks softly to
reassure her son, Beatrice quickly spoke   5
to calm my panting, pallid face.

"Are you forgetting you're in Paradise?"
she asked. "Forgetting how holy all of
Paradise is? How sincere goodness runs
through everything that happens here?   10
As you can see, things up here are too intense
for you. Can you imagine how you'd freak out
if you had seen my smile or if they were singing
right now? If you had understood their shouted
prayer, then you'd have learned that revenge will   15
come in your lifetime on the wayward monks below.
The sword of God comes when it may—too
slowly for those who want it, too quickly for
those who are afraid of it. But stop cowering
and take a look at all the souls around   20
us here. A lot of them are famous people."

I did as she told me to and around us I saw
a hundred stars sparkling, each one reflecting the
others so that they were all more beautiful together.

I stood in awe, restraining myself from   25
speaking even though I wanted to, afraid
that I might seem too eager or rude.
And, as if he sensed my desire to know
who he was, the biggest and most dazzling
of those hundred pearls came toward me.   30

"If only you could see into our loving hearts
around here," he said, "then you wouldn't
be afraid to speak what's on your mind.
But rather than wait for you and hold you
up on the way to your final goal, I'll answer   35
the questions that you haven't asked yet.

"The town of Cassino sits in the foothills
between Rome and Naples. An ancient temple
of Apollo once stood there, and the local people
worshiped at it. I am St. Benedict, the first one   40
to go up and teach those people about Jesus,
who came to Earth to bring the truths through
which man can reach Paradise. God's light
shone through me so strongly that it
turned those people from their pagan ways.   45

"These other flames," he went on, "were all
thinkers, men in whom the fire of pensive
contemplation smoldered, which warms
and nurtures the seeds of good deeds and
holy thought. This guy here is St. Macarius,   50
and this is St. Romualdus, and all these others
are brothers whose lives in sheltered monasteries
kept their hearts free from worldly distractions."

"Your kind words and the welcoming glow you're
giving off make me feel welcome and encourage   55
me to speak freely," I said to him. "It makes me
want to open up to you and take in everything that
you're telling me, like a flower turns toward the sun
and gathers its light. And so let me ask you, Father—
if you think I'm worthy of it—could you dim your   60
lights a bit and let me see what you really look like?"

"What you're hoping for will be given
   to you in the final Sphere, Brother,"
he answered, still gleaming. "There
   all longings reach perfection in their   65
   desire and only there are all desires
fulfilled, all yearnings calmed.

"That Sphere is beyond space and no poles divide it.
   But we do have a ladder that reaches the eternal heights,"
he said, gesturing, "though you can't see   70
   the top from here. It's the same ladder that Jacob
   saw in his dream, stretching up to Paradise
with the angels going up and down its rungs.

"But none of those on Earth nowadays make any
   effort to reach it," he sighed, "and the *Rule* I wrote as   75
   guidelines for monastic life is ignored, a waste of paper.

"The walls of the monastery are no more
   than dens of thieves these days, and the monks'
   robes are full of flesh as rancid as their meals.
But even the heavy interest they're earning isn't   80
   as insulting to God as their embezzling from the
   accounts that they're all greedily trying to tap into—
the monies collected by the Church are meant
   for those in need, those who ask for it in God's
   name, not for the monks' families and mistresses.   85

"Man is too easily corrupted. Just having
   a good start doesn't mean that an acorn's
   going to grow into a decent tree. Peter was
broke when he started out, and I never made
   a dime from all my praying and fasting.   90

Francis began his trip with humility, too. If you just
look at where we all were when we started out
and compare it to where our followers are now,
it's as different as black from white, night from day.
But whatever," he sighed. "God has fixed a lot bigger   95
messes than these, like when he parted the Red Sea
or stopped the Jordan River's flow for the Israelites."

And with that he floated back to join
the others and the whole cloud of them
whipped up and around and were gone.   100

So charismatic was her demeanor that,
with nothing more than a gesture, my
sweet Beatrice compelled me toward
that ladder. Up we went faster than you
could ever imagine traveling on Earth,   105
where every motion is hindered by gravity.

And let me tell you who are reading this
right now how much I would like to be up
there with all those guys in Paradise again!
We flew along and, faster than you'd   110
jerk your finger out of a candle flame, I saw
the stars of Gemini and was among them.

I owe all my talents—for whatever they're
worth—to the great forces of that glorious
constellation, my birth sign. The Sun rose   115
and set with Gemini in the skies on that
day when I took my very first breath of
Tuscan air, so it was fitting that at the
moment I was fortunate enough to

finally enter into the Heaven of the Stars 120
it sparkled there at my entry point as well.
From it, I hope, I'll be able to draw inspiration
and strength to go on writing about this
journey, just when the going gets toughest.

"You've almost reached the final goal," 125
Beatrice said. "From now on you'll
need a clear head and sharp eyes.
And so, before we go any farther,
stop and look down and see how far
I've brought you already. See the world 130
below you and be glad, so that you'll
be ready to meet the triumphant crowd
of souls who fill this ethereal Sphere."

I looked down through the Heavens and past all of the
planets we had come through until, far below, I finally 135
saw our little blue marble. It made me smile because it
seemed so puny. There is great value in the concept that this
spinning ball is nothing more than illusion, and those who
lean toward the other world reap greater rewards.

Far below I could see the Moon, and from this 140
side it didn't have any of the splotches that had
made me think it might have different densities.

And I could now look directly at Helios,
the Sun, son of Hyperion, with Mercury
and Venus spinning around him. 145

Above them I saw the mild Jupiter, orbited by
his father Saturn and his son Mars and from there
it was clear why they change position in our sky.

CANTO XXII, 151–154: IN THE HEAVEN OF THE FIXED STARS:
And far
below was that meager little speck of ours where
battles rage, all of its hills and cities and seas visible
in a glance from those eternal stars of Gemini.

All of the seven Heavens sparkled below me and
I marveled at their different sizes, their various   150
speeds, their distance from one another. And far
below was that meager little speck of ours where
battles rage, all of its hills and cities and seas visible
in a glance from those eternal stars of Gemini.

I turned my back on it all and faced her beauty eye to eye.   155

CANTO XXIII

ARGUMENT

In the Eighth Sphere of the Fixed Stars, Beatrice and Dante wait. Soon a brilliant light comes down from above, pulsing and outshining everything else. This is the glowing light of Christ Triumphant, and the vision is so intense that Dante can't stand it. But, strengthened by the experience, he can now endure Beatrice's full smile. Beatrice tells him to look around, and when he does he sees the Virgin Mary and the Prophets and Apostles. The light of the Archangel Gabriel descends around her and Dante watches as she rises up toward the highest Heaven, the Empyrean. All the souls sing "The Queen of Heaven," an Easter hymn, in her honor as she goes.

A young mother will sit quietly on the sofa,
watching her new baby sleep, feeling
safe in the home she's prepared
for him, and always keeping an eye out
for anything that could harm her son. Dawn   5
comes slowly through the window, and she's
happy to watch her baby wake, rubbing his
eyes and yawning, full of joy and expectation
to see the Sun bring in a new day.

Beatrice had the glow of that proud mother   10
on her face, a look of safety and happiness,
gazing straight up to high noon. I looked
at her standing there, full of hope and
anticipation, and I wanted to know what was up.
It gave me butterflies in my stomach.   15

Luckily, I didn't have to wait very long.
Before I could even say anything, I noticed
that the sky around us was getting brighter.

Beatrice turned to me then and said, "Here
you will see those who most believed in Christ,   20
directly blessed by Him without the filters of the
lower Spheres." As she spoke her face seemed
to glow, her eyes shining with a sacred
burning that I can't begin to put into words.

And like Diana, Goddess of the Moon,   25
surrounded by the sparkling lights of her
entourage of stars on a clear desert night,
I saw a brilliant light descend like the Sun,
hovering over all the others, igniting them
with its glow like our Sun sparks the stars.   30
A clear, glowing radiance pulsed out of
that light, so bright I couldn't stand it
and had to turn my bloodshot eyes away.

"Don't be surprised," Beatrice, my sweet, loving
guide began. "Nobody is immune from the light   35

CANTO XXIII, 31–33: THE VISION IN THE EIGHTH SPHERE:
A clear, glowing radiance pulsed out of
that light, so bright I couldn't stand it
and had to turn my bloodshot eyes away.

that is overwhelming you right now. No one.
Here is the wisdom and power that opened
the pathway between Heaven and Earth,
which mankind yearned for so desperately."

Like an over-inflated tire filled beyond its   40
limits, stretching until it can't stretch anymore,
finally exploding in one big bang, that's
how my brain felt as I stood there. Somehow,
I was beyond myself, I lost it, and now I can't
even really remember everything I saw there.   45

"Open your eyes and look at my smile," Beatrice said.
"You've learned a lot in all the places we've been and
now you should be strong enough to stand the sight."

When she said that I felt like someone who's just
woken up from a deep sleep, from a dream that you   50
want to remember but just can't quite seem to bring
it back in your head, your glimpses of it all foggy.
And I felt an overwhelming sense of gratitude, a
sense of debt I won't forget in a million years.

Even if the words I'm writing here could be   55
enhanced by the efforts of all of the poets
in history; even if all the most beautiful music
ever written was playing as you read this line,
it wouldn't even come close to conveying to
you the beauty of Beatrice when I turned to her.   60

And here is where the attempt at writing about
the things that I saw in Paradise runs into a
brick wall. It can't be done. I just have to leave
it at that and move on. And if you think about
what I'm trying to do, about how heavy this   65
whole topic is, you'll cut me some slack if I
mess up a little bit sometimes. This vast stretch
of ocean I'm paddling through now is no place for a
little canoe—and definitely no place for a timid sailor.

"Do I look so beautiful to you that you're   70
not even going to have a look around? Here
you are in the garden of Heaven, and here
blossoms Mary, the woman that gave birth
to Jesus, the flesh of God's word. And there are
the Apostles, who guided men toward good."   75

That's what Beatrice said to me, and I took her
advice, encouraged by her words. I faced the
full strength of the lights that had overwhelmed me.

Sometimes on an overcast or rainy day
you'll see a stray beam of sunlight cut   80
through the dull gray and light up a hillside.
There in Paradise I saw crowds of sparkling
jewels, glimmering and shining, lit
by some hidden spotlight from above.

O Jesus, light of my life, You ignite Heaven,   85
and raised Yourself to an even higher Sphere
so that my human eyes might see this place!

It was the name of the Virgin Mary, to whom
I pray every morning and every night,
that made me focus on that vision of fire.   90
And there before me I saw her, with all the
power of Heaven burning, radiating in Paradise
as it does down below. And as I watched,
a torch came down from above, spinning
slowly into a ring like a crown. It hovered   95
around her, wrapping her in its light.

As I watched I heard a song so beautiful
it'd make the most wonderful symphony
on Earth seem like the banging of a garbage
truck in comparison. The angelic notes floated   100
in the air around the Virgin, that sapphire jewel,
the brightest light in all the crown of Paradise.

"I am angelic love, circling the womb
of joy that once held Him, the hope
for all mankind," it sang. "I shall   105
surround you until you have risen
to the highest Sphere, following your
Son, blessing it with your presence."

And as the song ended, all of the
other lights of the souls in that Sphere   110
rang out with the name of Mary.

As she rose I followed her with my eyes.
Far above was the concave edge of the
dome of the Primum Mobile, the Ninth Heaven.
It's the most intense and breathtaking Sphere   115
that surrounds all of the eight Heavens below,
and it spins with the intensity of its closeness
to perfection. It was still too far away for
me to make out exactly what it looked like,
or to follow her rise as she sped upward.   120

Newborn babies will open their arms
after nursing, looking for their mother,
smiling with their love and happiness.
All around me the souls flickered as she
went, their flames stretching out after   125
her, so that their affection was easy
to see. *"O Queen of Heaven,"* they
sang, with such sweet voices that I'll
never forget how it made me feel.

If you could only see the rewards that   130
are waiting there in that Sphere for
those who are faithful to God in life!
Here they are able to enjoy all of
the rewards they earned while they
scorned material things and overconsumption   135
down below. And here, shining in victory and
holding the keys to Paradise, under the
glory of Jesus and His mom and all of the
Prophets and Apostles, St. Peter triumphs.

Avenue Station
Canto XXIV

CANTO XXIV

ARGUMENT

Still in the Eighth Heaven of the Fixed Stars, inside the constellation of Gemini, Beatrice calls to the souls for someone to come and meet Dante. From the spinning wheels of lights comes the flaming soul of St. Peter, chief disciple of Jesus, and holder of the keys to Paradise. He is considered to have spread Christianity to Europe after Jesus' death along with the Apostle Paul. Beatrice fittingly asks him to test Dante's faith to see if he is worthy of reaching Heaven's highest Sphere. St. Peter asks Dante three questions: What is Faith? What does Dante believe? Where did his beliefs come from? Dante replies to each and St. Peter counterquestions him until finally his answers are judged to be satisfactory. St. Peter hugs him in delight as all the souls sing.

Beatrice called out to the souls there: "Brotherhood
of the Chosen! You who share your table with
Christ, the Lamb of God, who feeds you until your
bowls are overflowing. Even before his life has ended,
this man here beside me has been blessed enough   5
to get a taste of that meal by gathering the scraps
that fall from your feast. Please, direct your attention
to him and be so kind as to quench his thirst a little, you
who drink eternally from the Source he so greatly desires."

As she said this, those sparkling souls formed   10
into several Spheres before us, spinning at different
speeds and flaming like comets in space.
Those wheels were like the cogs in an old clock,
each one propelling the next, but the largest of them
spinning so slowly that it was almost imperceptible,   15
while the smallest ones seemed to fly. And in their
dancing—each, it seemed to a different tune—their
speed and sparkle displayed to me their blessedness.

And then, from the circle that seemed to me to
be the most sacred, a soul came toward me,   20
sparkling with goodness more brilliantly than all
the others. He did three turns around Beatrice, the
whole time singing a song so amazing I just can't
remember it. I'm going to have to skip over it because
writing about it is pointless. Our imaginations—   25
and even more so, our language—could never
convey its complexities or render its subtle depths.

"Welcome, sacred sister. Your sincere
entreaties and devoutness have called me
from my circle so that I can come over."   30
That's exactly what that soul said
to Beatrice as he finished his song
and came to a stop before us.

"Eternal light of St. Peter," Beatrice answered,
"who was granted the keys to this amazing   35
place by our Lord, I ask that you test
this man on Faith, the very Faith that
allowed you to walk on water with Jesus.

"Ask him tough questions or easy ones,
whatever you want. Since you have seen   40
into the very face of God, I'm sure you
can tell by looking at him that he has Faith
and Hope and Loves well. But since Paradise
exists for those of pure Faith, it's only fair that he
should be called out so he can prove himself."   45

As I heard her saying this I did my best to
get ready, trying to organize my thoughts and
arguments in preparation for his questioning.
I felt like I was about to be challenged on my
dissertation, and stood quietly waiting for questions   50
from my thesis advisor, respectfully, with my head bowed.

"Speak up then, good Christian,"
I heard his voice say. "What is Faith?"
I raised my head and glanced at Beatrice,
who gave me a look that told me I better   55
put everything I had into my answer.

"Since I have been granted this opportunity
to address the Commander in Chief of the
Militant Church," I began, "I hope that I can
express myself properly. If I may paraphrase   60
the writings of your dear brother, St. Paul—the
one who, with you, set Rome on the road
to Christianity—then Faith is the substance

of things we hope for and the evidence of
things unseeable. That is the essence of Faith."   65

"That's correct," he replied. "But tell me,
do you understand why Paul listed Faith
as the first *substance*, or fundamental
principle, and then defines it as *evidence*?"

"The mysteries of Paradise cannot be seen   70
by mortal eyes as I can see them now,
nor can they be understood," I answered.
"Therefore, the existence of Paradise is a matter
of Faith; one's hope for Heaven depends on it.
This means that Faith is the foundation of Hope,   75
and this is why it's called a substance. Earthly things
are understood based on the evidence of the senses.
Heavenly things are grasped, lacking the senses,
on the basis of Faith. Therefore, Faith is evidence."

"Well," that soul exhaled affectionately,   80
"if everything that is taught down below were
understood so well, then we wouldn't worry
about those with unsound arguments. Since
you seem as familiar with these concepts as
you would be with a coin in your pocket, tell   85
me, do you have a quarter stashed away?"

"Of course I do," I said, smiling, "and it's as
bright and shiny as the day it was minted."

"So," the voice said from the depths of
that flame, "tell me, where did you get this   90
shiny coin on which all virtues are founded?"

"The texts of both the Old and New
Testaments, inspired by God Himself,
have proven to me beyond a doubt
that Faith has truth. Beside them,   95
all other arguments fall apart."

"So you're offering the Scriptures as reasons
for your faith," he replied. "But what makes you
think that they are actually inspired by God?"

"The proof of their truth to me," I said,   100
"is in the events they describe—miracles
that are not possible in the natural world."

"And how do you know that those things ever happened?"
he retorted. "The miracles can't prove the book is true
when your only proof of the miracles is the book itself!"   105

"If the whole world was able to be converted to Christianity
and the miracles never existed, then that alone would be a
miracle a hundred times more amazing. You yourself were
old and poor when you began your preaching, and even so
you were able to spread the seeds that bloomed into the   110
Church—although lately that plant's been a bit thorny."

And with that the whole crowd of souls burst out
singing the hymn *"Te Deum laudamus,"* echoing
through those Spheres with Heavenly melody.

Then Don Peter, who had been   115
stringing me along through that
discourse until we reached its full
blossoming, spoke to me again.
He said: "It appears that Divine Grace

CANTO XXIV, 103–105: ST. PETER'S QUESTIONING:

"And how do you know that those things ever happened?"
he retorted. "The miracles can't prove the book is true
when your only proof of the miracles is the book itself!"

has guided your thoughts and so far   120
you have expressed yourself well and
in convincing form. I approve. But now
I'd like to know what it is that you believe."

"Dear Father, who can now see here
in Paradise that which you believed so   125
strongly on Earth that you outran John
when you both rushed to Jesus' tomb,"
I answered, "you're asking me to explain
my unwavering faith and how I came
to it. Well I'll say this: I believe in one   130
God—unique and eternal. One who
moves Heaven and Earth with his love.
As a basis of this I have both physical
and metaphysical proofs. And I have the
truth as it flows down through the writings   135
of Moses and the Prophets and the
Psalms and the Gospels and through your
own writings about what Jesus said to you.

"And I believe in the Holy Trinity—that
they are one thing and at the same time   140
three, both singular and plural. And
again, the nature of this condition
of God has come to me through the
Scriptures. They are the spark that
lights the fire, the breath on the   145
glowing coals that now burn
inside of me like a star."

And as I finished speaking old
St. Peter embraced me like a teacher
does his student on graduation day,   150
both of them happy. Then he started
singing again and spun around me
three times, because he was so
happy about everything I'd said.

CANTO XXV

ARGUMENT

The canto begins with Dante expressing his hopes for his life on Earth: that his poem will be worthy and influential, that he will be able to return from exile to his native Florence, and that someday he will be recognized as a great poet—crowned with the poet's laurel in the Baptistery of San Giovanni, where he was baptized as a child. A second light now approaches from the ring of souls. It is St. James, a disciple of Jesus, who asks Dante three questions about Hope: What is it? Where does it come from? How did it come to you? Sensing that the second question might be hard for him to answer since it might make him appear arrogant, Beatrice jumps in on Dante's behalf and states that no living person has as much Hope in his heart as he. Dante answers the other two questions, and all the souls sing. The gleaming soul of St. John then approaches, and in his curiosity to discover whether it's true or not that St. John ascended to Heaven in his human body, Dante stares into the brilliant light. St. John tells him that the only humans to rise to Heaven in human form were Jesus and Mary, and Dante suddenly realizes that he has gone blind.

If it so happens that this poem of mine—which
Heaven and Earth had a hand in writing, and which has
made me lose weight from the effort of scribbling it—
if it ever wins over the hearts of the cruel Black
Party that has exiled me from the streets of my   5
Florence, then I'll return with grayer hair and
a more mature voice in my writing. I'll return
home as a *bona fide*, meaningful writer, and
I'll accept the poet's laurel wreath with honor
at the Baptistery of San Giovanni, where I first   10
was welcomed into Christianity—the faith that
made St. Peter circle above me way up there.

A new light now came toward us from that
ring of souls of those whom Christ had left
to be his vicars, and of whom St. Peter was   15
the first of all. "Look, look," Beatrice said,
"here comes St. James, the one whose
grave in Spain attracts so many pilgrims."

And like two old friends who hadn't seen
each other in a long time, who smile and   20
hug and pat each other on the back in
happiness and affection, I watched as those
two great saints embraced, sparkling in delight,
praising the feast that Paradise provides.

When they had finished their elaborate greeting,   25
they stopped in front of me and they both burned
so brightly that I couldn't bear to look at them.

"Dear, illustrious James," Beatrice began, smiling,
"who described the generosity of Paradise
in your writings—please do the honor of   30
discussing Hope now. You are the most qualified,
as you were its symbol when Jesus singled
you out with Peter and John among His disciples."

"Lift your head and relax," I heard him say
to me. "Everything that comes to Heaven   35

CANTO XXV, 19–23: THE APPEARANCE OF ST. JAMES:
And like two old friends who hadn't seen
each other in a long time, who smile and
hug and pat each other on the back in
happiness and affection, I watched as those
two great saints embraced.

CANTO XXV

above from the Earth below must ripen in
our light." And so I lifted my eyes to those
souls of St. Paul and St. Peter before me,
whose radiance had made me bow my head.

"God in all His grace and wisdom has   40
decided that even while you are still alive
you are to meet His Dukes in Paradise
itself, so that by seeing the truth here, you
might be reassured in Hope, and thereby
reassure others. And so tell me then: What   45
is Hope? How did it come to grow in you?
And where did it come from?" Those are the
three questions that St. James asked me.

And before I could answer, Beatrice, who had
guided and steered my course on this whole   50
flight so far, guessed my answer and said:

"There is no living Christian who has
more Hope in his heart than he does, as is
evident in the light of God's will, which we
all can see. That is why he's been allowed   55
to come from Earth to visit Paradise even
before his struggles are over down below.

"The two other questions you asked are not
for your own sake, I know, but so that he can
tell the world later how much Hope means to   60
you. I'm going to let him answer them on his
own, as they're pretty easy and he won't have
to brag. May God's grace help him reply."

As I responded, I felt like a student answering
his favorite teacher in a subject that he'd been   65
studying for months and knew by heart.

"Hope is simply the expectation of making it
to Heaven, which is given through God's
grace to those who have earned it," I said.

"I know this from all the reading I've done
and the people I've met along the way. But it
originally came to me through David, King of
Israel, whose Psalms speak a lot about Hope.
'May all those that know You, have Hope in You,'
he wrote. And with me being a Christian, of course
I know Him. It was from those first drops, added
to by the writings in your Epistle, that the
first trickle became a flood of understanding."

As I spoke, I saw huge flashes going off
inside the light of St. James like lightning,
until finally he said, "The love I still have
for the virtue of Hope has burned in me
ever since my martyrdom and my escape
from the battle of life. Now it flares again at
hearing the words of someone like you, who so
obviously loves this virtue. Please, tell me, what
will Hope bring to your life in coming years?"

"Both the Old and New Testaments talk a lot
about the ultimate destination of those who
follow God," I said. "To me, that destination is
what is promised by Hope. Isaiah says that those
in Heaven will wear the double garment of glorified
body and soul, and that the land they inhabit is
Paradise. And in Revelations, your brother, St. John,
writes clearly about the luminous bodies of the blessed—
how the soul lasts forever and the body is purified."

As soon as I had finished speaking
I heard the souls above us sing out
"Sperent in te" as all the dancing lights
seemed to agree with me. And one of
the lights in that crowd became so
brilliant that if the constellation Cancer
had even one star that bright, it would light
the wintertime night sky as if it were day. And
like a good friend who is so happy for his buddy

70

75

80

85

90

95

100

105

on his wedding day that he forgets about
himself completely, I saw that light rush over
to Peter and James and join them as they
hovered in the air. And there it joined the
celebrations with the other lights, as Beatrice   110
watched, silent and calm, taking it all in.

And as she watched them she spoke
to me over her shoulder. "The new one
is St. John," she explained, "who hugged
Jesus at the Last Supper and whom   115
Jesus asked to watch out for His mother,
Mary, as He hung dying on the Cross."

When you're a kid and you don't know any
better you might try to stare at the Sun during
an eclipse instead of using a shade, which is   120
safer. There I was, squinting into the light of
St. John, until I heard him say, "Why are you
trying to see something that doesn't exist up here?
My body is buried down on Earth with
all the others until the Final Judgment   125
Day comes. Only Jesus and the Virgin Mary
were allowed to rise up to Paradise in
their original bodies. Feel free to make
that clear when you write it in your poem."

The instant he spoke the entire mob   130
of lights up there had frozen in place,
silent, their songs ended, harmonies gone.
It was that startling, instantaneous silence
of a bustling restaurant when a wine glass
drops and shatters in a loud pop.   135

In that sudden stillness I turned to look at Beatrice.
Can you imagine how shocked I was when I
realized that I couldn't see anything at all, even
though I was with her right there in Paradise!

CANTO XXVI

ARGUMENT

Still in the Eighth Heaven of the Fixed Stars, St. John reassures Dante that his blindness can be cured, and then begins questioning him on the virtue of Love. When Dante answers successfully, the angels rejoice, and his sight is restored with a glance from Beatrice. Besides the three souls of Saints Peter, James, and John—representing the Theological Virtues of Faith, Hope, and Love, respectively—there now shines the soul of Adam. Dante is surprised to meet the first man and asks him four questions that Adam answers: Why was he kicked out of Eden, exactly? How long did he live? What language did they speak in Paradise back in the day? And, how long did he get to hang out in Eden before being evicted?

As I stood there panicking at being
blinded, I heard the voice of St. John
coming to me again and I focused on it.

"Since you have spent your powers of sight in
looking at me, let's see if you can compensate   5
for its loss by using your brain. To start with,
I ask you this: what is the ambition of your
soul? And don't worry, your sight is not lost, only
obscured. The woman who has been guiding
you through these sacred regions has in her eyes   10
the power to heal your sight, just as Ananias
healed St. Paul's when he got to Damascus."

"In that case, I hope that sooner or later her
healing reaches my eyes, those doors to my heart
that have burned for her since I first saw her," I   15
answered, relieved. "As for your question about
Love: God is the beginning and end, the Alpha and
Omega of all Loves, from the highest to the lowest."

And the same voice that had first
consoled my fears about my vision now   20
replied in a way that made me concerned.

"That may be," I heard him say, "but be
more specific. What was it that has directed
your love toward God, since, apparently,
it hasn't always been so focused."   25

"By my philosophical ponderings and by
the visions I have seen here," I answered.
"They have made a lasting impression on me.
Goodness, once it is understood by the mind,
inspires Love by itself, and the greater the   30
good the more intense the Love. Anyone
who can grasp this simple truth must
naturally be moved to Love—to God's Love
more than any other—since His is the
highest form of it. Any Love besides   35
His is just on offshoot, a reflection, of it.

"This concept is clear to me," I went on, "made
clearer by Aristotle, who explained that it is
natural for the soul to want to exist, and since
its existence comes from God, for the Love of   40
the soul to be for God. God said the same thing
when he told Moses, 'I will show you all Goodness.'
You yourself confirmed this in the beginning of
your book when you explained the nature of God
to all men more clearly than others' books do."   45

"So," I heard him say in my blindness,
"by way of reasoning and the authority
of the Scriptures you have concluded
that God is the source of all Love.
But tell me if you feel any other   50
leads drawing you to that conclusion."

I knew what that Eagle, St. John, was
driving at. It was clear what kind of
answer he wanted to hear from me.

"Everything combines in me to steer   55
my love toward God," I insisted. "The
simple existence of the world and me
in it; the death of Jesus on the Cross for
my sins; and that which everyone who
believes hopes for—Paradise itself!   60
All that, together with the stuff I already
mentioned, have anchored me firmly in
directing my love toward Him. It's not tossed
around in the stormy seas of human loves anymore.
Now I wander the streets of the world loving   65
all things as He has intended them to be."

And as I concluded my explanation I heard
the voices of all those souls, and Beatrice
with them, sing out, *"Holy, holy, holy!"*

If you're dead asleep at night and someone   70
comes and turns on the light, it will wake
you up. That orange glow hits the inside

CANTO XXVI, 91–93: MEETING ADAM:

> "Wow, Adam!" I said. "You're the only
> man ever to be created full-grown! Our
> oldest ancestor!"

of your eyelids and races toward your brain
so that you sit up, confused, and don't know
where you are for a second until you sort things
out and it all comes back to you. That's what
Beatrice did to me, gazing at me with that
thousand-mile stare of hers and suddenly
I could see again, even better than before. I stood
there dazed, blinking, and asked her about the
fourth light I now saw in front of us.

"In that flame, burning with Love, is
the first soul ever created by the
Primal One," she said. "This is Adam."

When I heard that I bowed quickly,
like one of those plastic drinky-bird
novelties or like a bobbing oil well
on a hill. I was still disoriented by the
blindness thing, but getting my sight
back gave me a surge of confidence.

"Wow, Adam!" I said. "You're the only
man ever to be created full-grown! Our
oldest ancestor! The guy to whom every woman
is a daughter and every groom a son-in-law!
Hey, can I ask you a couple of questions?
Wait. I'm sorry. I'm talking too much. You go."

Sometimes when I'm playing with my dog
I'll throw an old towel over him. Even
though you can't see him you can see him
moving around under it. Well, I couldn't see
Adam either, through all that glare, but I
could tell he was happy by how he moved.

"Even though you haven't asked yet," he said,
"I already know what you're going to ask
better than you do. All things created are
reflected perfectly through Him, even though
nothing created is a perfect reflection of Him.

75

80

85

90

95

100

105

"What you're dying to know is how long it's been
since I was in the Garden of Eden, where your
guide there prepared you for your climb up here.   110
And you want to know how long I lived there, and
what really happened to get us evicted. And finally
you're wondering what language we spoke back
in those days and how we came to learn it.

"Well son, I'll tell you that despite what you think   115
it wasn't the apple-eating that was so bad, it was
the fact that we'd broken the rules—we wanted
to be better than we were—that got us in trouble.

"After that I was sent to Limbo—where your
buddy Virgil is now—and I was there for four   120
thousand three hundred two years, dreaming
of this place the whole time. On top of that,
I lived to be nine hundred thirty before I died.

"The language we spoke back in those
days had disappeared even before King   125
Nimrod started building his tower in Babel—
which he never got around to finishing. You
see," he explained, "nothing created by man
lasts forever. Through use and fate it gets tinkered
with. People are naturally designed to speak, but   130
how you do it, and in what language, is left for you
to make up—and believe me, it won't be English only.

"Before I died and was sent to Limbo in Hell,
'I'—'jah' was how we pronounced it, like reggae—
was the name we had for God, and later   135
he was called 'El' in Hebrew. Times change.
Things come and go like trains at a station,
like seasons. One thing dies, another grows.
As for the Garden of Eden, the entire time that
I got to spend up there on top of Mt. Purgatory   140
was less than one day—from dawn until around
noon, when the sun has passed its peak."

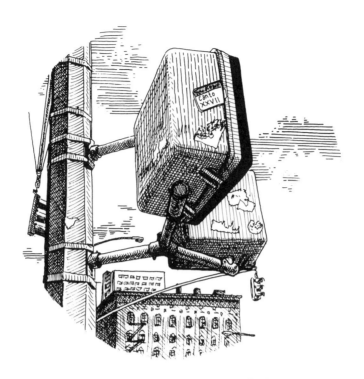

CANTO XXVII

ARGUMENT

Dante is ecstatic, still in the Eighth Sphere of Paradise. Surrounded by souls, he watches as the gleam of St. Peter burns brightly and turns from white to red. Peter goes into an angry tirade against Pope Boniface VIII and other corrupt Popes, and against the state of the Church since his death. When he's finished, at Beatrice's urging, Dante again looks down through all of the Spheres of Paradise that they have visited and sees Earth far below. When he looks back at her, he realizes that they have risen to the Ninth Sphere, the Primum Mobile. She explains that this Heaven contains all of the other Spheres below and is itself contained within the Empyrean, the highest Heaven. Finally, Beatrice laments the perversity of mankind, who turn away from the spiritual to chase after worldly goods, and says that it won't be long now before Fate intervenes.

"*G*lory *be to the Father, to the Son,*
and to the Holy Spirit," sang all the
souls up in Paradise. It was beautiful.

At that moment, standing there with Adam,
the whole universe seemed like one big party   5
and I was drunk on Paradise punch. I had that
rush of happiness you get sometimes,
when everything seems perfect, that life is full
of love and peace, and I had everything I wanted.

The four burning souls of Peter, James,   10
John, and Adam hovered before me,
radiant in the brilliance of their light.
Gradually, Peter seemed to glow from white to red
until he sparkled like the planet Mars or like
an Emergency Exit sign in a dark theatre.   15

In Paradise, God's loving-kindness runs
everything, and when the time had come
for that whole crowd to finish up their
song, I heard St. Peter say:

"Don't be too concerned about my change in color,   20
because as I speak you'll see all the others change too.
Pope Boniface VIII, who stole my place—my place!
my place as Pope on Earth!—is so corrupt and
useless that in the eyes of Heaven that seat is as
good as empty! He has turned Rome—where I lie   25
buried—into a stinking sewer of blood, into the kind of
town where Lucifer himself would feel right at home."

And as he spoke I saw that whole Sphere
glow reddish orange, like clouds at dawn
or evening when the sunlight strikes   30
them. I glanced over at Beatrice and
saw her face flush, not out of shame
for herself—she was too good for that—
but like one who is embarrassed for another.
(They say that a shadow like that passed over   35
the Sun when Christ was on the Cross.)

St. Peter continued then, but in a voice
much different from what it had been.
It was the biggest change I'd seen in him.

"I gave my very blood—as did my   40
successors, Linus and Cletus—for the
Church herself, not for financial gain!" he
said. "Popes Sixtus, Pius, and Urban all
suffered and died for the Church as well,
to achieve their place in Paradise.   45

"We never wanted our followers to be divided
in any way, some over here, others over there!
We never intended for the keys that I was
entrusted with by Christ Himself—now a symbol
on the papal seal—to emblazon banners that are   50
carried into battle against other Christians! I never
asked for my face to be used on the stamp that he
uses to seal his indulgences and other shams! It pisses
me off and embarrasses me when I think about it!

"From up here it looks like all Shepherds below   55
are nothing but wolves to the flocks they should be
tending! Oh, God, why do you hold back your power?

"Popes John XXII and Clement V from
Gascony are already planning their schemes!
After such strong starts, how low they have   60
fallen in the end! But Providence will soon bring
help for Rome, as it did for Scipio and his
army in his victories over Hannibal, I'm sure.

"And you, my son—whose human body will drag you
back down to Earth when you're finished here—make   65
sure you tell everyone what you heard from me!"

And like a snowstorm in winter, the
season of Capricorn, I saw the air filled
with glowing flakes in that Sphere of Heaven.
As I watched, thousands of glowing souls   70
began to rise toward the Empyrean, returning
above after they had appeared to us there.
I watched that gleaming snowstorm of

souls as they rose, higher and higher, until
they had disappeared into the distance.   75

Beatrice saw me watching them go and
said gently, "If you look down now, you'll
be amazed to see how far we have come."

Far below us I could see Cadiz, and I realized
that we had crossed six time zones since I   80
last looked down. Far to the west I could
see beyond the Straits of Gibraltar, where
Ulysses' crazy trip took him, and far to the east,
I could almost make out the shores of Phoenicia.
I might have been able to see more of that   85
meager speck of ours except for the motion
of the Sun beneath my feet as it moved
westward into Aries, leaving the east in
shadow. But my mind was focused on
Beatrice, and I turned my eyes toward her.   90

If you were able to combine all the beauty
of nature and everything that art could
invent to seduce our eyes and snare our
minds, it would seem like nothing in
comparison to the divine glow that shone   95
from Beatrice when I looked at her face again.

The beauty of her radiance was more than
enough to pull my thoughts from the stars
of Gemini below and focus my attention now
on Heaven's fastest Sphere. This new realm   100
was so alive with movement and so beautiful
that I can't really say at what point we
entered it. But Beatrice, her face glowing
with the new light of this higher Heaven,
saw my doubts and rushed to calm them.   105

"The entire universe is, by its nature, perpetually
revolving," she explained, "and this is the still point
of its central axis. This Sphere, the Primum Mobile,
is contained within the Empyrean, inside the
very mind of God Himself—the source of the   110
love that fuels the turning of the Heavens below.

CANTO XXVII, 85–87: THE VIEW FROM THE HEAVENS:
*I might have been able to see more of that
meager speck of ours except for the motion
of the Sun beneath my feet.*

"Light and love surround this Sphere just as
it surrounds the Spheres below, and only He
who encloses them understands how it works.
The motion of all the Heavens is generated   115
here, its turning is what spins all the others
down below. It's the engine of the universe.

"And since time is a principle of motion, and the
motions of the Heavens are visible from Earth,
you'll see that time has its roots here as well.   120

"Oh, Greed," she lamented then, "You seduce
mankind into your swirling waters so that none
have the strength to avoid your undertow.

"Like any seed, all men bear the promise
of healthy fruit when they are young.   125
But the rain of the years rots the fruit
on the vine. Faith and innocence are
only pure in children, and both are
gone by the time a boy starts to shave.
In the babble of infancy one is content,   130
but by the time he can speak the child is
already hungry for the things of the world.
As a child he loves and obeys his mother's
voice, but as soon as he can speak for
himself, she's as good as dead to him.   135

"That's how it always happens.
Long exposure to the Sun will burn
even the purest soul. And this is no
surprise, since there is no one below to
govern the world as it should be,   140
and mankind wanders astray.

"But don't worry: well before a
thousand years have passed, Providence
will set those lost ships on the true
course, turning their bows to where   145
their sterns are now, until the whole
fleet is steaming toward safer harbor.
Then the blossoms of man will finally bear fruit."

CANTO XXVIII

ARGUMENT

Looking at Beatrice, Dante sees a glimmer reflected in her eyes. When he turns to look behind him, he sees God as a tiny, brilliant point of light. Around that light spin nine rings, like a mini—solar system, one for each of the Angelic Intelligences, the Orders of the Angels. But, unlike the Heavens that they have already visited, Dante sees that the closer the ring is to the center, the faster it spins. Beatrice explains that in the material world of the Heavens where they are now, the Spheres' scale corresponds to the amount of blessedness each contains, so that the higher Spheres are bigger and spin faster. But in the spiritual Heavens that they're looking at, the rings reflect the love and energy of God, and therefore the smallest ones glow brighter and spin faster, since they're closer to God. She then names them in descending order, and says that Dionysius, the early Athenian theologian, had it figured out from Earth, but only because St. Paul helped him out a bit.

Once Beatrice, that girl who fills my
head with thoughts of Paradise,
had explained the truth to me I saw
how far wrong the pathetic views of
people in the world can be. And as   5
she stood there explaining it I saw
in her eyes—those eyes of hers that
suck me in with so much love there's
no escape—I saw a light reflected, like
headlights in a store window, and   10
quickly, without even thinking about it,
I spun around to see it for myself.

As I turned I saw what anyone else
would see if they looked intensely
at the Sphere of the Primum Mobile   15
as it spins through Paradise. I saw
a point of light so piercing—like the
brilliant white of a welding torch—that
anyone who looked at it would have
to shut his eyes; any star in our sky   20
would have seemed pale beside it.

There was a ring of lights around
that brilliant point, like a halo, kind of,
or like the ring around the Moon on
a foggy night. That ring glowed and   25
spun faster than anything I'd ever
seen on Earth or in all the Heavens.

And that ring was circled by another
and another. I counted six rings
around that point, and outside of them   30
was a seventh circle so big that if you
doubled a rainbow into a circle it
probably would have been smaller than it.

Finally, there were two more circles, the
eighth and ninth, and I noticed that the   35
biggest ones were moving the slowest,

CANTO XXVIII, 9–12: IN THE NINTH SPHERE:
*I saw a light reflected, like
headlights in a store window, and
quickly, without even thinking about it,
I spun around to see it for myself.*

being farthest from the point. I guessed
that the closest ones must be more pure,
since they were nearer the Pure Source.

"From that point all of the Heavens and   40
the Earth depend," Beatrice said when
she saw how confused and anxious
I must have looked. "If you look at
the circle closest to it, you'll see its
whipping around by the force of its love."   45

"It looks almost like a small version of
the solar system," I said. "That would
make sense. But what's bugging me
is that what I've seen of this place is
the opposite: the smaller Spheres like   50
the Moon spin slower than the bigger,
outer ones do. And the farther out we
go, the more divine each Sphere gets.
So if I'm going to really understand
this place, I'm trying to figure out why   55
the mini version is the opposite of
the big one. I really don't get it."

"It shouldn't surprise you that you can't
unravel the mystery," she answered.
"People have been trying to figure out the   60
connections between the physical and the
spiritual for ages. But since you want to know,
then pay attention while I explain it to you.

"The circles in Paradise that we've
visited have their blessedness distributed   65
equally throughout them. Therefore, the
more blessed, the bigger each one has
to be to contain it, so that the Primum Mobile,
where we are now, is the biggest and spins
the fastest. But the circles you   70
see now are measured by the
power each contains, not by their size.

Thus the smallest ones spin faster since
they're closest to the Source of their power.
They contain the Angelic Intelligences;   75
each ring has one Order. So you see
there's a perfect correspondence
between the two, it's just reversed."

Her explanations cleared the storm
that had been gathering in my head   80
like the northeast winds that sweep
the skies over Italy, pushing away
the clouds and letting the Sun shine.
And the clear truth of what she
said sparkled like a star on   85
those clear, summer nights.

When she had finished speaking, as
if on cue, the lights of those rings each
exploded, like fireworks, into a jillion
gazillion sparks, all of them   90
sparkling at once and racing around
the rings with the rest. And from those
gleaming millions I heard a song bust out,
from ring to ring, singing *"Hosanna"*
to that fixed Point of Light that holds   95
them forever where they've always been.

Beatrice must have seen in my face that I wanted
to know more and said, "The angels of the first two
rings are of the highest orders. They are the Seraphim
in the first orbit, and the Cherubim in the second.   100
They are nearest the Point because they are most
similar, most inspired, and most propelled by it.

"The angels of the third ring are called the
Thrones, since they round out the first group
to three, and they reflect the divine judgment of God.   105
And I should point out that the blessedness
of each of the rings reflects the depth of their
view of God, the Truth that satisfies all

doubts. And so you can see that blessedness
results first from vision and then from love, since you   110
must see—or understand—something in order
to love it. Love is a result of comprehension.
So the bliss of the souls is in proportion to
how deeply they see, and their merit is
shown by the intensity of their radiance.   115

"The second group of three rings that you
see in this place of eternal spring—
which never fades when Aries the Ram
comes along in the fall—those rings
sparkle in eternal celebration and song.   120
Their group is made up of the Dominions,
then the Virtues, and last the Powers.

"And in the next, outermost group of three
you have the Principalities, then the Archangels,
and finally the Angels we all know and love.   125

"All of these Orders are focused up toward God,"
she explained, "and the power they exude is directed
downward, each pulling the next ring toward the center.

"Dionysius, through much contemplation, was
able to discern these Orders and named them   130
properly in his book *De coelestia Hierarchia*.
Pope Gregory I disputed him and got their sequence
messed up in his book *Homilies on the Gospel*,
but when he got up here and had a look for himself
he smiled at his own mistakes. And it shouldn't   135
surprise you that Dionysius was able to figure
it out from down on Earth—St. Paul told him
about it from up here, about their sequence
and some other stuff about these rings."

CANTO XXIX

ARGUMENT

Still in the Primum Mobile, the Ninth Sphere, Beatrice contemplates the brilliant gleam of God Himself. She then speaks to Dante, answering his unasked questions about the Creation and the nature of angels. She explains that God created the angels and the Heavens and the prime matter of the universe simultaneously, despite what others have written, and she discusses the fall of Lucifer and the other angels who rebelled against God. She explains the nature of angels and their numbers, and ends with a long tirade against the false teachings of vain priests on Earth.

When the Sun is in Aries and the Moon is in
Libra, then one rises while the other sets, at
opposite places on the horizon. There is a
brief moment when, if you look from one to the
other, they seem to be balanced like a scale,   5
each one half-obscured as it rises or sets.
For just such a moment Beatrice stared silently
at that brilliant Point of Light, smiling, after I
was forced to turn away from its intensity.

"Now I'll tell you—not ask you—what you   10
want to know," she said, "as I see it plainly
in that place where all begins and ends.

"God created everything spontaneously, on a whim,
sort of, since He is perfect and didn't need to do
anything. He wanted His creations to reflect His light   15
and to savor their own existence, as He does. And
so in the eternity beyond time He blossomed into new
things. The angels were the first things created.

"And it's not like God wasn't doing anything
before He created the angels, because there was   20
no time, and so there was no such thing as 'before.'

"Pure form, pure matter, and a blend
of the two all were created at once,
simultaneously, like pellets from a shotgun.
When you turn on a light switch all the lights   25
in the room come on at once, without there
being one before the other, with no time
between the switch and the light itself. That's
what it was like. Form, matter, and their
mixture all flashed into existence in a moment.   30

"Everything that was created instantaneously
had a place and an order: Angels, the pure act,
belonged at the top of the universe. Mankind,
pure potential, came at the bottom; and in the
middle were the Heavens, the planets, and stars—   35
created from the blend of pure act and pure potential.

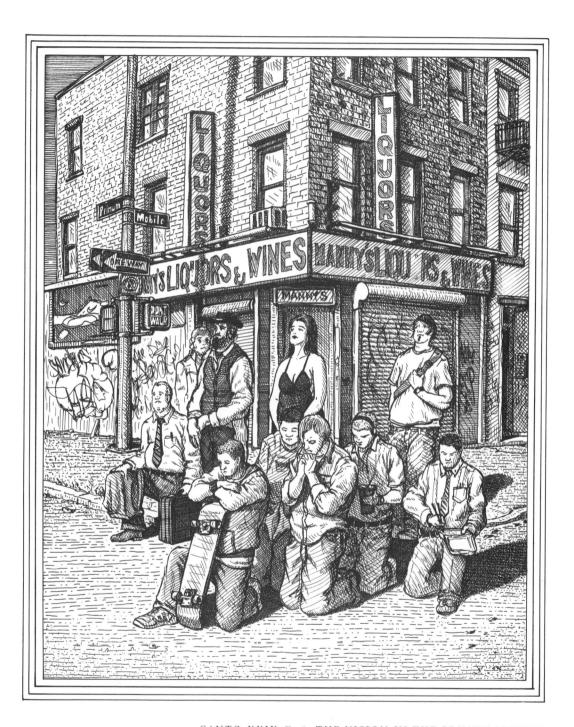

CANTO XXIX, 7–9: THE VISION IN THE PRIMUM MOBILE:
*Beatrice stared silently
at that brilliant Point of Light, smiling, after I
was forced to turn away from its intensity.*

"St. Jerome wrote in his commentary that the angels
were created before the rest of the world,
but that's kinda not really how it all happened.
If you look at the Bible carefully, you'll see   40
that it talks about the Creation differently, like
how God created everything at the same time.
Logic helps us here, too: the angels give movement
to the Heavens, and they had to be created at the
same time—so they had something to move.   45

"So now you know when, where, and how
all the angels were created; three parts
of your questions have been answered.

"But things went wrong. Before you could even
count to twenty, Lucifer led about a tenth of the   50
angels in revolt, only to be cast down to Earth, creating
the pits of Hell in their fall. The rest of the angels
remained where you see them now, happily serving their
purpose, working their art in harmony and pleasure.

"The rebellion began with Lucifer   55
whom you have already seen below,
imprisoned in Hell by the weight of the
world. When it was over, all of the angels
that you see around us now realized that
their patience and humility would be   60
rewarded with the vast grace required to
do their work moving the Heavens. Their will
is now tied to His through that understanding.
And so you can see, if you haven't already,
how the rewards of His grace are in proportion   65
to how much you want to receive them.

"By now, if you've been paying attention,
you shouldn't need much more from me to
comprehend what you see around you.
But since down on Earth you still teach   70
in your schools that it is the nature of
angels to have memory, understanding,

and will, I'm going to explain things
further so that you can see how the
truth has been confused by teachers.   75

"Remember that from the very first moment
of their creation, these angels have never
turned away from the all-seeing face of God.
Nothing has ever come between them. So then,
they have no need of memory, since there   80
is nothing for them to remember but Him.

"Down on Earth, people have daydreams
and aspirations, hoping for things both
good and bad (though the latter is
despicable). Down below you follow many   85
paths in life as you grow—your philosophizing
and love of material things often carry you astray!

"But while your vanities raise eyebrows
up here, it's the disdain and distortions
of Holy Scripture that really irritates.   90
People forget how much blood was spilled
in spreading His word around the world, and forget
how honorable is the man who is focused on God.

"Your preachers are more concerned with their
own words than with His, more interested   95
in showing off than spreading the truth!
I've heard some preach that the darkness
at the Crucifixion was caused by the
Moon reversing its course and causing
an eclipse! And some say that the effect   100
was visible as far away as Spain and India,
when that's not the case at all, it's a lie!

"Fables like these are spread from the
pulpits all the time! There are more lies going
around down there than Smiths or Joneses.   105
The result is that the people come back from
church with nothing more to think about than hot
air. But even so, ignorance will not save them.

"Jesus didn't stand there and say to His disciples,
'Go forth and preach trash to the whole world,'   110
but gave them building blocks of truth and love.
The disciples had Jesus' words in their hearts
and they went to war to keep that faith alive,
with the Bible as their only sword and shield.

"Now men are happy to preach with dirty   115
jokes and bad puns as long as they get
a couple of laughs to feed their egos.
If people could only see the beast hiding
beneath those robes they would see the
lies behind the pardons they are granted—   120
pardons that only increase the gullible nature
of the people, who continue flocking to the
Church for more meaningless indulgences.
Some monks are filling their checking accounts from
people's pockets, and there are even worse pigs   125
out there, paying their bills with false promises!

"But I've gone on too long," she said,
sighing. "We should focus on what's
in front of us before we run out of time.

"The number of angels that exist is greater   130
than any number imaginable," she said.
"It's beyond human understanding. And if you
look again at what the Prophet Daniel wrote in his
book, you'll see that while he talks about there
being thousands of them, he doesn't get very specific.   135

"The brilliant glow of God shines down
through all the angels, illuminating them
all in many diverse and varied ways. And
since each receives God's light differently
they all express it differently, too—some blaze   140
brightly away, while others simply glow.

"And now you have seen the true scope—the width
and breadth of His eternal Goodness. He has made
so many mirrors of Himself, each with its own light,
but He still remains, as always, the One."   145

CANTO XXX

ARGUMENT

As they watch, their view of the Point and its encircling rings of light fades, and Dante turns to Beatrice. She now grows exponentially more lovely as he watches, surpassing any Earthly description. The two rise to the final Sphere of Paradise, the Empyrean. This is the outermost, all-encompassing realm of God Himself that exists beyond all things. In awe, Dante sees a river of light flowing through flowery fields of gems being pollinated by hovering sparks from the river. This is the grace of God and the sparks are angels in service to the souls of the redeemed. Beatrice tells Dante to drink from the stream so that he can see the reality of Paradise, beyond its metaphors. He does, and now all is transformed into an enormous, endless stadium that rises like a yellow rose, filled with angels and saints, and lit by the light of God from above. Almost all of the seats are filled already (Dante and his contemporaries felt that the end of time was near), but Beatrice explains that one of the empty seats will be filled by the soul of Emperor Henry VII, who will rise to power in Italy and attempt to put an end to factional fighting there. He will fail, due to the opposing influence of Pope Clement V, whom God will punish by sending him to Hell where he will suffer with his predecessor Boniface VIII, whom Dante met in the Inferno.

In the early morning hours when the Sun
is still a quarter of the world away and the
shadow cast by our Earth is long, gradually
the dome of sky above begins to change
and the dimmest stars fade away. As   5
dawn comes, preparing the way for the
Sun, she creeps around turning off the lights
one by one, until finally even Venus,
the prettiest one, is gone for the day.

Gradually, like the dawn, the riot of   10
lights that swarmed around the Point—
which at once embraced them and was
also their focus—began to fade from
my sight. When I could see nothing
more, I turned to Beatrice in wonder.   15

Even if everything that I've ever said about
her could be gathered together and crunched
into one sentence, that sentence would be
useless in describing how she looked right then.
It was a beauty God Himself created, utterly beyond   20
anything I could think of. Only He could fully appreciate it.

I give up! At this point in the poem, I'm
more at a loss for words than any case
of writer's block ever struck a poet.
Just the memory of her smile at that   25
moment blinds my thoughts like how
vision goes all white when you look at the
Sun. From the very first day I ever
saw Beatrice's face when I was nine, until
that moment there, I have never stopped   30
thinking about her. But now I'm struck mute.
Dumbfounded. There's no point in my trying
to write another word of description about her,
I'm tapped out. I'm nearing the end of this
difficult theme anyway, so I'll leave it to   35
some writer better than me to toot her horn.

And she, in all her beauty and with the voice and
demeanor of a guide, said to me: "We have now

left the largest material Sphere, the Primum Mobile,
and entered the Empyrean, the Heaven of pure light.   40
It is the pure light of the intellect, of love, of Goodness,
of Truth, filled with happiness beyond all bounds.
Here you will see two groups—the angels and
the saints—which will appear to you in the bodies
they will re-inhabit on Judgment Day."   45

Suddenly I was surrounded by darting lights
so strong that I was overwhelmed and couldn't
follow anything with my eyes. It was like lightning
in the dark or when a flashbulb goes off in
your eyes, making things so momentarily   50
clear that you can't see anything else for a while.

"Love, which holds this realm still and calm, always
welcomes newcomers like that," she explained,
"so that each new spark is ready for the fire."

As soon as I heard her words I had the   55
sensation that I was rising, or being pulled up,
by a force not my own. And as my eyes cleared
from the flash I felt that my sight was now
stronger, sharper, that no light, however bright,
could obscure my vision again. And now I saw   60
a river of light—red and gold—like city streets
seen from above during Christmastime, and its banks
were blooming in glorious spring flowers.

From that river of light, swarms of sparks
popped out from its surface, hovering like   65
bees and landing on the flowers so that
each one twinkled like rubies set in gold.
Then the sparks shot off again and dove
back into the river and another took off.

"The excitement that's burning inside you   70
to see everything and to understand what
you see makes me happy as I see it welling
up inside you," said Beatrice, the light of my life.
"But before we go any farther, you need to take
a drink from this stream to satisfy that thirst."   75

CANTO XXX, 60–62: THE EMPYREAN:
And now I saw
a river of light—red and gold—like city streets
seen from above during Christmastime.

"Everything you're seeing—the river, the
flowers, these topaz sparks popping up
all the time, the gold grass waving—these
are all merely shadows of what they really are.
It's not that these things are incomplete or unripe;   80
it's you who aren't yet ready to see them as they truly are."

When I heard that, I rushed toward the
stream faster than a hockey player toward
the net on a breakaway, trembling, wanting to
get its power so that I could see clearly.   85
On my knees I drank from that brook that
flows for the improvement of humankind.
And even as I drank I saw the stream
before me begin to change, widening into
a circular pond, a lake, as I gulped.   90

Then, like at a Halloween party when everybody
takes off their masks and are much better looking
than they were before, those flowers and sparks
I watched transformed completely. I rose up
and stood surrounded by the saints and   95
angels who inhabit the courts of Paradise.

(Here I must ask God's help in describing
what my eyes saw there, the awesome glories,
the elation of the true land of Paradise.)

From high above the light of the Creator of all things   100
is revealed to His creations, granting them a peace
that can only be found in Him. The light is
so vast that it would easily surround the Sun.
It is so bright that you can only see its reflection
bouncing back off the dome of the Primum   105
Mobile, passing His light onto the Spheres below.
Its power and motion and influence are such that all below is
a reflection of Him. And like the many reflections in
dressing room mirrors—where you look and see
yourself many times—I saw a thousand tiers   110
surrounding the light, reflecting it like seats in a

vast stadium descending in a circle. And in them
I saw all of the souls who have won their place in
Paradise, returned there from their exile below.
The lowest rows were closest to me, and even those   115
were so huge that I couldn't imagine the enormous
scale of that place, that rose of light, to the highest seats!

But from the farthest to the nearest
I could see clearly, with my new, improved
eyes, sweeping across the expanse and   120
taking it all in. Up here, things like distance
and haze don't exist, because in Paradise
the laws of nature are unnecessary.

Beatrice now led me into the yellow glow of
that enormous rose, whose levels rise and   125
open like petals, fragrantly, blossoming for the
Sun in the perpetual spring. I followed, in awe.

"See," she said, beaming. "I knew you'd like it!
Welcome to Paradise! See how big it is? Look
how far up it goes! See how everyone wears white?   130
And look, almost all of the chairs are filled,
we're just waiting for a few more to arrive.

"I see you're looking at that one seat, the empty one
with the crown over it. Well, before you get up here
to this wedding banquet that place will be filled. It's   135
reserved for Emperor Henry VII. He's destined to
set Italy back on track, but unfortunately, she won't
be ready for him. You Italians are blinded by your
own greediness; you're always biting the hand that
tries to feed you and you'll starve because of it.   140
And when Henry gets to Rome, Clement V will be
Pope and—either openly or in secret—he'll oppose
his reforms. But just wait and see! God won't put up
with Clement for very long before He sends him
down to that ring of Hell where Simon Magus suffers.   145
Clement will be stuffed right into the same
hole as his predecessor and will shove
Boniface VIII deeper in as he does."

CANTO XXXI

ARGUMENT

Dante contemplates the hosts of Paradise in the Empyrean, beyond all the Spheres, spread out in a giant amphitheater before him like a white rose. Angels fill the air, hovering over the souls, and Dante is dumbstruck. He turns to ask Beatrice a question but finds that she's gone, replaced by St. Bernard, who explains that he has been sent to guide him through the rest of his journey. Beatrice has taken her seat in the third row from the top, and Dante can see her across the vast distance with his renewed strength of vision. Bernard directs him to look even higher, and there on the top row sits the Virgin Mary, Queen of Heaven.

And now I saw spread before me like a pure white
rose all the souls of Paradise—the Elect, the souls of
women and men married to Jesus through His sacrifice.

Around them, flittering and spinning, hovered
the crowd of angels, eternally singing to   5
God's glory, in praise of the goodness
that makes them sparkle. They were
like a swarm of brilliant bees, darting
into the flowers and out again, filled with
pleasure at their own work. Together, they   10
all flew down into that enormous rose, and
then soared back up to the Source of all love.

Their faces glowed almost like living flame, their
wings were made of gold and their other parts were
whiter than an early morning snowstorm. As they   15
dove into that flower, zipping from row to row,
they spread the peace and passion they
had gathered, their wings beating in the air.
And even though there were so many of them
buzzing around between the ranks of that   20
rose and the light above it, their numbers didn't
cast any shadows. God's light penetrates
the universe to all things according to their
worth, and nothing can shade His glow.

That amazing kingdom of joy radiates   25
the happiness of those saints, souls from both
ancient and recent times, all focused on Him.

Oh triple light from the Sun that shines in their
eyes up there, making them so happy! Don't forget
us down here in our storms below!   30

Traveling south from their lands where
both the Big and Little Dippers mark the
reaches of the sky, the Barbarians were
astounded when they reached the city of
Rome. Its huge plazas, amazing monuments,   35

and palaces struck them dumb. So imagine
what I felt: I had come up to Heaven from human
Earth, had traded in my wristwatch for celestial
time, went from corrupt Florence to peaceful
Spheres. Dazzled as I was by the spectacular   40
view and the rush of emotion, I stood there
amazed, taking it all in, unable to say anything.

Exhausted climbers, on reaching the summit, are
filled with a rush of energy and emotion that they
often find hard to describe to others. Standing there   45
in Paradise I let my eyes wander over that stadium
of souls, from row to row, up to the highest seats
and back down to the lowest, trying to drink it all in.
Everywhere I looked I saw faces filled with love,
glowing with His light as well as their own smiles,   50
their every gesture full of dignity and grace.

And after I had gotten over my initial
shock and had some time to look around,
glancing over the whole layout but not
really focusing on anything specific,   55
I turned to Beatrice, my brain full of
questions and things I wanted to ask.

But there was somebody else where
I expected her to be. Instead of my girl
there was this old guy, dressed like all the   60
others, standing there with an expression
of happiness on his face as he looked
at me like a father looks at his son.

"Where is she?" I asked, slightly startled.

"Beatrice sent me," he said smiling. "She   65
asked me to leave my seat and help you on
the final leg of your trip. If you look way up
to the top, third row down, you can see where
she sits from here. It's the seat she's earned."

CANTO XXXI, 45–48: THE ROSE OF HEAVEN:
Standing there
in Paradise I let my eyes wander over that stadium
of souls, from row to row, up to the highest seats
and back down to the lowest, trying to drink it all in.

I didn't say anything but looked up   70
where he told me to and saw her
sitting there, a crown above her head,
reflecting the eternal light. The distance
between us at that moment was farther
than you would be from the clouds even   75
if you were at the bottom of the deepest
ocean. But even that far away I could see her
perfectly, as crisp and clear as satellite TV.

"Dear lady," I prayed in thanks as I looked
at her. "I've relied on you for so long. For   80
my sake you ventured into Hell, and through
your strength and power I've been able
to see and understand everything that has
passed in front of my eyes. You led me from
the bondage of evil into the freedom of God's   85
justice by all these paths we've traveled, by
all the ways that are in your power. Please,
remember me in your generosity, so that
when the time comes for me to return,
my soul will be one that you welcome."   90

And even though she was super-far
away, she looked down at me and
smiled, then turned back to God's light.

"In order that you reach your chosen
destination," the old guy began, "I've   95
been sent along by both prayer and
love to help you. Take a good look
around. The things you see here
will help prepare you for God's light.
The Virgin Mary, whom I've worshiped my   100
whole life and beyond, will give us what we
need, as I am her most devoted: Bernard."

People all over the world know the *Mona Lisa,*
the world's most famous painting, and everyone
has an idea of what it looks like. But when   105

they travel all the way to Paris and finally
see it in the Louvre, they always do a double take.
"Is that what it looks like?" they think.
That's how I felt when I looked at St. Bernard,
who spent his life in contemplation 110
and devotion to the Virgin Mary.

"Dear Son," he said, "if you want to
understand this place you have to
look to the highest rows, not the
lowest ones. There you will see 115
the Virgin Mary, Queen of Paradise,
the one to whom this Sphere is devoted."

As I raised my eyes up across those
rows it was like looking from west to
east at sunrise—the whole place 120
seemed to brighten as I turned my
head until I finally saw one place at the
highest row that was brighter than all the
rest. And just like the dawn, when the place
on the horizon where the Sun is rising is 125
the brightest and the glow fades off at
either side, the radiance at that highest
point was the strongest, and the gleaming
of its flame faded away around it. And hovering
around that gleaming point were more than a 130
thousand angels with their wings outstretched,
each one different than the others.

And there, right in the middle of everything,
sat the Virgin Mary, whose smiling beauty was
reflected in the eyes of everyone around her. 135
And if my words were even close to what I
remember, I still wouldn't even try to write
down the smallest part of her splendor.

When Bernard saw me staring at her
with such awe and devotion, he turned 140
to her too, with so much love on his
face that it made me look even harder.

CANTO XXXII

ARGUMENT

In the Empyrean, St. Bernard shows Dante around Paradise. He explains the seating arrangements of the souls and saints in the rose-shaped arena, including such figures as Mary, Mother of Jesus, St. John the Baptist, and Adam and Eve. The souls are arranged in specific ways: one side for those from before Jesus' time who believed in the coming of Christ, and one side for those who believed in Christ after His death. A large area is reserved for the souls of dead children, and Bernard explains that they must arrive through Jesus or end up in Limbo. When Dante seems doubtful, Bernard insists that the justice of God is unknowable, but that it is fair. Finally, after pointing out all the famous people, Bernard tells Dante that he should get ready to see God Himself, and that he should ask Mary to prepare him. "But I'll do it for you," he says, and Bernard begins to pray.

Even though he had been all caught up in his admiration
of Mary and just enjoying being in Paradise, St. Bernard
was happy to take the time to show me around.

"See Eve over there sitting at Mary's feet?"
he asked. "She was the cause of the wound   5
to mankind that Mary was able to heal. Below
Eve, in the third row seats, you can see Rachel
and your favorite, Beatrice, side by side.
Going down from there you can see Sarah,
Rebecca, Judith, and Ruth, the great-grandmother   10
of King David, who wrote 'Have mercy on me, God'
in his Psalms after regretting his adultery with
Bathsheba. Keep up with me here as I point
them out, row to row, petal to petal, in this rose.

"Now from the eighth row down you'll see   15
a whole line of Hebrew women sitting who
kind of act as a dividing line in this whole
big flower here. On your right side, where
the rows open up near the top, sit all those
souls who believed in Christ even before   20
He was born. (You can see that all those
seats are filled already.) Now on your left
is where all the souls sit who believed in
Him after He died. Notice that there are
quite a few empty seats there, reserved for   25
the people who haven't gotten here yet.

"Now if you turn around and look behind
you you'll see that this dividing line carries
across and up the other side, stretching
from the throne of Mary, over to the throne   30
of St. John the Baptist up at the top on
the other side. He had to hang out in the desert,
eat bugs, then be martyred, and then spend
two years down in Hell just to get here! Now
coming down from him you can see Francis,   35
Benedict, Augustine, and rows and rows of
others until you get back to the center here.

"So you can see how fair and good at
planning God is," Bernard continued,

"because he divided this place up equally,
    girls over there, guys over here, sort of.
    And that's not all: All of the lower seats
    are for those souls who died young, as
    children, before they had the power to
    distinguish right and wrong for themselves.
    But you probably already had that figured
    out by yourself, just by looking at
    their faces and hearing them sing.

"Oh, but now I can tell you're dubious," he said
    looking at me. "You're just not saying anything.
    But hold on a sec and I'll clear it all up for you.

"See, in this whole, huge place no one ever gets up here
    by luck. Everything has a place, just like there's no room
    for anything bad up here—like hunger or sadness.
    Everything you see is here by the will of God, and He's
    nothing if not fair. Everything fits up here—from the clothes
    they give you to your seat. The hand fits the glove, so to speak.
    And that means that even these kids are here for a reason,
    as per their merits. Just as every person in the world is
    different, kids are too, and so there's some reason why they
    each sit where they do. The Guy up there," he said, pointing,
"who's responsible for this place and for all of us in it, the
    Guy who makes us all happy so that you couldn't ask for
    anything more, He's got His plan, He knows what He's doing,
    and He spreads His rewards around in a lot of different ways,
    however He sees fit, and that's pretty much all there is to it.

"And that shouldn't surprise you at all," he added.
"You can see the whole kid thing played out
    between Rebecca's twins, Jacob and Esau.
    It's written there in the Bible. God's grace
    falls on people in as many different ways
    as there are colors of hair in the world.

"Since kids haven't really distinguished
    themselves in life yet, only God knows the
    reasons why they're ranked as they are.
    In the earliest times of the world, children
    used to come to Paradise through their own
    innocence, or because of their parents' faith.

40

45

50

55

60

65

70

75

Later on it was necessary to circumcise
all males to cleanse them for Paradise.   80
But once Jesus had lived and died,
since then baptism has been necessary
for kids to come up here. Without it,
they have to go to Limbo.

"And now take a good look at Mary, and   85
you'll see where Jesus got His looks. Only
her radiance can prepare your eyes for His."

I looked up to where Mary sat, and from
her face there beamed so much love and
goodness that it overwhelmed me and took   90
my breath away. She seemed to soak up all
of the goodness of those holy angels surrounding
her, who had been created for that very reason.

And as I watched I saw the most radiant angel
fly over and hover in the air before Mary on open   95
wings. *"Hail Mary, Full of Grace,"* he sang and the
whole crowd in that sacred stadium joined in
the song. All together they sang, beautifully,
and each one's face shown with admiration.

"Father, please," I began, "I already owe   100
you big-time for coming down here from
that sweet seat you've got up there just to
show me around a bit. But please, who is
that angel hovering there, looking right into
her eyes? I can see him gushing so much   105
he's glowing." So once again I had to ask for
guidance from that guy who shone beside
me like the morning star, reflecting Mary's glow.

"That guy is our most charismatic angel, and
for good reason. He's the Archangel Gabriel,   110
the one who was sent to appear before Mary
with the palm of victory, announcing her divine
pregnancy. Her child was the Son of
God, and He accepted the burden of our sins.
But pay attention now and follow along with   115

CANTO XXXII, 88–90: THE VISION OF MARY:

> *I looked up to where Mary sat, and from*
> *her face there beamed so much love and*
> *goodness that it overwhelmed me.*

your eyes and I'll point out some of the
other people in this sacred auditorium.

"Way up there on either side of Mary sit two guys
who are pretty much the foundations of this whole
place. You can tell they're happy with the seats they've   120
got. The guy there on her left is the father of us all,
Adam, whose brash apple-tasting left a bad taste in
the mouth of all humanity. And on her right you can
see St. Peter, the old guy there scratching his nose.
He is pretty much the father of Christianity, and Jesus   125
gave him the keys to this whole place, to all of Paradise.

"Beside Peter you've got St. John. He's the guy that
had all those visions of bad times to come for the Church
and he wrote about it in his Book of Revelation—all the
troubles even after the sacrifice of Jesus, what with the   130
nails and spear, etc. Now on Adam's left you can see
Moses, who led the Jews out of Egypt into the desert,
where they had to eat manna, all of them complaining and
changing their minds and never thanking him for anything.

"On the far opposite side, facing Peter, you can see   135
Anna way up there. She's Mary's mom, so proud of
her that she sits there smiling and staring at her. And
opposite Adam you've got Lucia. Don't forget she's
the one who sent Beatrice down to help you out.

"But, hey, time's flying. You're tired and we can only   140
squeeze so much juice out of a lemon, you know.
So let's get you a look at the Big Guy, huh? Let's
hope your eyes are strong enough that you can
get some idea of Him and what He's all about.

"But just so you don't falter and wobble in these   145
last steps of yours, you need to ask for a final
little boost from Mary. She's the one who can
help you out, if anyone can. I know how to deal
with her so you just let me do the talking. But pay
attention, so that my words come from your heart."   150

And with that he started to pray.

CANTO XXXIII

ARGUMENT

St. Bernard offers a prayer to the Virgin Mary, and describes Dante's journey to her. He asks her to strengthen Dante's vision so that he can endure the sight of God Himself. Dante looks up to see the Divine Light as a burning brilliance, and within It he sees the unity of all Creation and all of time. As he stares into the Light he sees that It contains three Spheres of different colors, all the same size. As he watches, the human form of Christ appears in one of the Spheres. While he struggles to comprehend this blending of the human and the divine, he is struck by an instantaneous flash of understanding and enlightenment. Here his memory fails, and he is left with the sensation of his will and his desire surrendered to the love of God.

"Virgin Mary, the daughter of your own Son,
you're the most humble and celebrated of all,
as you were God's entryway into this world;
you are the one that made human nature
noble enough so that God, who created man,   5
wasn't unwilling to become a man Himself. The
love of God was rekindled in your womb, and
its warmth has germinated this flower
inside the eternal peace of Paradise.
Up here in Heaven, you are the noonday Sun   10
of love, while down on Earth, men see you
glowing as the symbol of eternal hope. Lady,
you are so amazingly powerful that whoever
looks for grace without your help may as well
try to fly without wings. Not only do your   15
sweet blessings rain down on those who
ask for them, but often you send kindness
without even waiting for a request. In you there
is charity, in you there are pity and tenderness,
in you there is generosity, in you is what unites   20
all that is good in the living things of this world.

"Here is a man who has come from the
deepest pits of Hell to these heights of Paradise,
who has heard many stories and seen many souls
along the way. Now he asks you to be kind enough   25
to give him strength so that he will be able
to look up and see the final vision that heals all
things. You know I've never wanted
anything more than I now want this. All my
prayers and desires are that he may now see it—   30
and I hope my prayers move you enough
to clear the lens of his mortality, so he can
see the Sum of Joy revealed in all Its splendor.

"And finally, Mary, you who can reach
every goal, please keep his heart pure   35
after he sees and returns to Earth. Shield
him from all those mortal passions.
Do you see how even Beatrice and the saints
around her are joining my prayer to you?"

Mary's eyes, loved and cherished by God,   40
looked at Bernard as he finished, and
you could tell how much she appreciated
his words. Then she turned and raised her
eyes to the Eternal Light—the Light no
other being can see as clearly as she.   45

There I stood, at the end of the road, at
the verge of obtaining the desire of all
humankind. I lifted my eyes to follow hers.

Old Bernard was smiling at me,
signaling for me to look up, but I   50
had already lifted my head. My vision
became clearer, more pure, and I
could see into the brilliant gleam,
into the Light that is Truth Itself.

What I saw in that Light is beyond   55
the ability of words to describe, beyond
the limits of my mind to remember.

Sometimes you can have a dream that's so
intense you'd swear it was real, and when you
wake up you can't remember any of it. That's what   60
I feel like now. My memories of that sight are almost
completely faded from my head, but the intensity of
the emotion I felt is as sweet now as the moment
I stood there. They fade like footprints in the sand,
like the words of the ancient Sibyl, written on the   65
leaves that blow away in the wind in Virgil's *Aeneid*.

Dear Light Supreme, burning so far beyond
all human understanding, please help me to
remember some of Your appearance, and help
me to find words eloquent and true enough to   70
convey even one spark of Your fire so that
I can convey my experience to future generations.
If You can return to my memory and inspire
the rhymes of even a few lines of this poem,
I'll be better able to explain what You are.   75

CANTO XXXIII, 46–48: THE VISION OF GOD:

There I stood, at the end of the road, at the verge of obtaining the desire of all humankind.

DANTE'S PARADISO

The blinding Light that I endured was so
intense that I think I might have lost my
way again if I had turned away from It.
I can remember that this fear was
what helped me to keep my eyes   80
focused until I reached the Infinite.

With generous thanks I accepted that
Eternal Light into my eyes for so long
that my vision was completely obsessed.

In Its depths I saw all the elements of the   85
universe that seem separate and scattered,
united into one place, bound together and
connected by love. Substance, accidents,
events, emotions—everything so intertwined
that my simple description seems useless.   90

I think that in the tangle in front of me, I actually
saw the universal form that fuses all things—even
as I write I'm filled with a rush of certainty.

That one moment is more fuzzy in my mind
than all of the forgotten details in the twenty-five   95
centuries since Jason's ship startled Neptune.

All of my being was focused in that moment—
deeply, intensely—as I gazed at that Light.
And the more I looked the more I wanted to see.

Anyone who sees that Light is transformed   100
so that it becomes impossible for him to
be distracted by anything else. The goal
of everyone's desire is shining there in such
perfection that everything else afterward
seems to be defective, distorted somehow.   105

And even though I remember bits of it, my
feeble descriptions of that vision are as
useless as gibberish in describing it.

God is eternal and unchanging, simply
One. He is as He always has been.   110
But as my sight grew stronger the
longer I looked, it seemed that the
Light changed as I stared—even though
I knew It didn't, my vision changed.
In that clear and depthless Light, I now   115
saw three circles, all the same size but
different colors. One circle seemed to
reflect the other, like a rainbow
within a rainbow, and the third seemed
like a flame shining from the first two.   120

But the power of words is pathetic compared
to the power of thought! And the word "pathetic"
is too good to describe the failures of this poem.

O Eternal Light, focused only on You, known
only by Yourself, and by so knowing, You   125
glow and radiate love, both knowing and
being known! As I watched, the circle that
You fathered gleamed inside You like a
reflection and gradually I saw the image
of Your Son inside of it, glowing the same   130
color as its ring, sparkling with the image of
man, until all my attention was focused on it.

I stood fixated on that fantastic vision
before me, struggling to understand the
incomprehensible like a math student   135
grappling with the quantity of π. I wanted to
see and understand how that human image
fitted that circle and found its place there.
But it was beyond me, baffling. And then
suddenly, out of the blue, it came to me in a   140
flash of light, and I understood completely.

And here force fails my intellect; but my
will and my desire had been set in motion—
like a perfectly balanced wheel—driven by
the Love that moves the Sun and the other stars.   145

CANTO XXXIII, 139–141: DANTE IN PARADISE:
And then
suddenly, out of the blue, it came to me in a
flash of light, and I understood completely.

ACKNOWLEDGMENTS

"Words without pictures never to Heaven go."

That sentence would be considered a rather loose adaptation from Shakespeare's *Hamlet*. And while for the past four years Marcus Sanders and I have played fast and loose with adaptations of what a few folks consider to be some of the most sacred of texts in world literature, whatever our shortcomings (which may be extravagant) our words and pictures were never composed without a great deal of thought and intention. Now here we are in Paradise.

You might think that after slogging through the depths and muck of Hell and then climbing a mountain that *Paradiso* would be some kind of cakewalk. It wasn't. In fact, it was just as difficult as any of the other parts of this journey, if not harder. (Although the lighting was nicer.)

Again, most of our thanks on the path go to Brother Michael Meister, our Virgil, who did not abandon us at the doors to the Garden of Eden but carried on advising, overseeing, and editing through the ten heavens. He has guided us through the mists and fogs of dogma and literature and politics and mythology and astronomy and geography and poetry. Patiently.

We also feel much gratitude toward Noah and David and everyone at Trillium Press; Catharine Clark and her gallery in San Francisco and Eleana Del Rio and her gallery in Los Angeles; Alan Rapp, Leslie Davisson, and Stephanie Hawkins at Chronicle Books; Peter Hawkins for his enthusiasm and Mary Campbell for her thoughtful kindness and time; Wendy and Penny at P.P.O.W. Gallery in New York for taking a leap of faith in the project; Nick Debs and Choire Sicha, also in New York; Susan Landauer and Ann Wolfe at the San Jose Museum of Art; Heidi Donner and Carrie Brewster at St. Mary's College; Shea, for sharing his paradise in Tahiti; Jamie Brisick, Vavâ Ribeiro, and Noah Elkin for sharing their thoughts and sofas in NYC; and finally, obviously, to Elyse. Thank you all for everything.

Dante's Paradiso isn't what we'd expected. But in some ways it's been even better. Cheers. —SANDOW BIRK

"Heaven is a place where nothing ever happens." —TALKING HEADS

Additionally, I'd like to thank Matt Warshaw for his advice and encouragement; Matt Walker for his ongoing heckle; Jade Hays, Marcos Cortez, Paul Piscopo, and Marlin Lum for their distractions; and Heather Goodman for love and support. —MARCUS SANDERS

COLOPHON

ABOUT THIS EDITION AND THE DIVINE COMEDY PROJECT

This book is the trade edition of Sandow Birk and Marcus Sanders's *Dante's Paradiso*, originally published as a limited-edition, leatherbound book by Trillium Press in 2005. The Trillium edition is illustrated by sixty-nine hand-pulled original lithographs from drawings by Birk, and was printed in an edition of 100. Trillium has published deluxe editions of *Inferno* and *Purgatorio*.

Trillium Press is a collaborative printmaking workshop located in Brisbane, California. Since 1979 Trillium has been producing fine art limited-edition prints with established, mid-career, and emerging artists. Trillium graciously provided the prints from which this Chronicle Books edition was created.

Prints and paintings from *Paradiso* debuted at P.P.O.W. Fine Arts, New York, May 26–June 30, 2005, and will be included in San Jose Museum of Art's major exhibition of the complete *Divine Comedy* from August 27, 2005–January 8, 2006.